Nicknames

Social Worlds of Childhood

General Editor: Rom Harré

Nicknames
Their Origins and Social Consequences

Jane Morgan
Christopher O'Neill
Rom Harré

Routledge & Kegan Paul
London, Boston, and Henley

First published in 1979
by Routledge & Kegan Paul Ltd
39 Store Street, London WC1E 7DD,
Broadway House, Newtown Road,
Henley-on-Thames, Oxon RG9 1EN and
9 Park Street, Boston, Mass. 02108, USA
Set in 10 on 11 pt IBM Press Roman by
Hope Services, Abingdon, Oxon.
and printed in Great Britain by
Lowe & Brydone Printers Ltd
Thetford, Norfolk

British Library Cataloguing in Publication Data

Harré, Romano

Nicknames. — Social worlds of childhood.
1. Children — Language 2. Nicknames
I. Title II. Morgan, Jane III. O'Neill, Chris
155.4'18   LB1139.L3   78-41077

ISBN 0 7100 0139 8

Contents

General Editor's Preface

For most of us childhood is a forgotten and even a rejected time. The aim of this series is to recover the flavour of childhood and adolescence in a systematic and sympathetic way. The frame of mind cultivated by the authors as investigators is that of anthropologists who glimpse a strange tribe across a space of forest and millennia of time. The huddled group on the other side of the school playground and the thumping of feet in the upstairs rooms mark the presence of a strange tribe. This frame of mind is deliberately different from that of the classical investigators of child psychology, who have brought adult concepts to bear upon the understanding of children's thoughts and actions, and have looked at childhood primarily as a passage towards the skills and accomplishments and distortions of adults. In these studies the authors try to look upon the activities of children as autonomous and complete in themselves. Of course, not all the activities of childhood could be treated in this way. Rather than being in opposition to the traditional kind of study, the work upon which this series is based aims to amplify our understanding by bringing to light aspects of childhood which usually remain invisible when it is looked at in the traditional way. The ethogenic method is in use throughout the studies represented in this series, that is the children themselves are the prime sources of theories about their actions and thoughts and of explanations of the inwardness of their otherwise mysterious activities.

Prefatory Note

To set the nicknaming practices of children in a larger framework we have been obliged to make some study of the socio-psychological role of names in adult life. Rudimentary though these have been we feel that they suggest a great number of unsolved problems for future investigators to look into. We are only too aware how much remains to be elucidated in the field of nicknames proper, and how speculative are many of our conclusions. We hope that others will be encouraged to put us right.

By suppressing clues to the real-life identity of our participants we hope we have spared any embarrassment to those who have very willingly helped us. We are particularly grateful to Mansur Lalljee, Riq Anderson, Yumiko Ishikawa, Jonathan Bye, Sarah Davis and Amin Baidoun for their help in empirical studies.

Social psychology, we believe, should entertain as well as instruct. To that end we have included various snippets and odds and ends that would have been excluded from the old sober-sides 'scientific' social psychology.

J.M., C.O.'N., R.H.

1
Theoretical Introduction

The Social Psychological Importance of Childhood

The discussions in this book are to be seen in a sociological framework which distinguishes the social development of human beings, at least in complex, non-tribal societies such as ours, into three phases, in each of which a social order obtains which is both psychologically and sociologically distinct.

First Phase

Until about the age of five a human being lives in close symbiotic relationship with adults, particularly with its mother or other prime caretaker. The child's rudimentary social skills and cognitive operations are completed by contributions from the mother, which gradually decline in importance as the child gains the capacity to do these things for itself. For example, close analysis of a mother's speech with an infant shows her to be ascribing to, and thus creating for, her child a rational systematic flow of intentions, to interpret his strivings as the meaningful actions of a fully developed human being (Richards, 1974). This is connected with the synchronous process between mother and child that Bruner has called 'fine-tuning' (Bruner, 1977). Gradually a child takes over these functions for himself (Shotter, 1979). There are two people present when a mother and her child are together. One is the mother, the other the mother-child, the symbiotic unit created by the mother's continuous completion of the child's activities by incorporating the marks of a fully rational being, namely intentions, wants, plans and the like. An infant, then, is always, socially speaking, embedded in an adult world.

As Bowlby (1971) has so convincingly demonstrated, the tie that binds these individuals and symbiotic pseudo-individuals into a strongly interacting system is emotional in character, based upon the effective consequences of attachment and loss. The social world built up on these ties is a dependent world, dependent on adults for its form and functioning.

Second Phase

We are convinced that from the age of about five a new mode of social functioning develops with a quite different psychological basis, which creates a society or rather a multiplicity of societies which are relatively independent of the influence of adults. These social orders form an autonomous world, which is bound together by ritual and convention. It depends upon the interpretation of symbols, and it is controlled largely by verbal formulae and other linguistic means. For instance, property is obtained and retained with verbal formulae such as 'Baggsie', friendships are ritually ratified with rhymes and the formal exchange of symbolic gifts, games are made orderly by rhyming schemes for turn-taking, and so on.

This social world has three outstanding characteristics.
1 Its structure is created by ritual and maintained by convention, just as the adult social world is created and maintained.
2 Emotional ties and drives are severely subordinated to the power of the rituals. They may even be used in a contrived way in the setting up of such activities as games, where ritual insults are used to generate conventional emotions of rage and resentment which are formalistically expressed and relieved in games of chase (Sluckin, 1978).
3 Personal qualities, both of appearance and behaviour, become a serious issue. Correct ways of being are promulgated and deviations sanctioned according to ideals which have little or nothing to do with adults' ideals for those very same children at those ages.

As the Opies have shown (Opie and Opie, 1959), the forms and relationships, techniques of control and so on of the autonomous world are strongly conserved, over literally hundreds of years. The forms and practices of this world are reproduced from one generation of children to another and apparently relatively unaffected by and immune to adult influences. It is our contention that the lineaments of the adult social world are mainly laid down in the children's autonomous social world, not in the official educational institutions wherein yet another social system prevails including both adults and children with its own rituals and conventions. We are inclined to believe that the influence of the autonomous world far outweighs even that of the family, which declines quite rapidly, so far as we can see, as the child enters into independent relationships with children of his own age.

Third Phase

Sometime in late adolescence this autonomous social world gives place to the societies of adulthood. In the adult world ritual and convention are still the dominant mode of the formation and maintenance of social relationships. Emotional ties are largely ephemeral and, unless they are ritually ratified, tend to dissolve (Harré, 1977). So the machinery of the adult world is, in many respects, like the machinery of the autonomous world, and draws upon the same socio-psychological skills of verbal and other symbolic rituals and the capacity to see through to the symbolic value of a thing or an action. The transition to the adult world occurs through replacement of content. New ideals of personality and even of physical appearance make themselves felt, and are mostly promulgated by quite different processes from those of the autonomous world. Yet in the autonomous world the main outlines of acceptable ideals of appearance and behaviour have already been strongly inculcated.

We believe that where it exists it is the nicknaming system above all that is the effective instrument of the social control of personal appearance and personality projection in the autonomous world. We will be offering some suggestions as to the social conditions favouring the development of nicknaming systems, but we are unable to say how the control of personality is effected in childhood sub-worlds lacking this institution.

But before we turn to our detailed exploration of nicknaming we would like to draw the reader's attention to one consequence of the general theory of social development we have just outlined. If we are right, the theory explains the extraordinary resistance of modern societies to deliberate and contrived attempts to effect fundamental social change and to reform social relationships. These attempts have taken one or both of two forms: an attempt to bring about social change by modification of economic relationships, or an attempt to reform the educational institutions. Both attempts have been justified by reference to theories about the genesis of adult social relationships, the former depending on the theory that social formations are re-flections of, or perhaps even caused by, the structure of the economic system, the latter on the theory that much of the reproduction of social forms takes place in school. The former touches adult social relation-ships long after they have been formed in the autonomous world of childhood. The latter may affect the classroom society—but as we argued in *The Rules of Disorder* (this series), the classroom is more the source of criminal behaviour than it is a nursery of social morality. It is in the knot of giggling girls, in the scrum of boys scragging an offender, in the sudden outburst of a running chase, all of which are *on the other side of the playground*, that the bones of the social structure are to be found. Studying nicknames is one way we can get a glimpse of these profoundly important apprenticeships to social competence. Only when we understand the way ritual skill and interpretative and symbolic action are learned will we be in a position to suggest how they may, for agreed moral purposes, be modified.

Personality and Character

In our contacts with other people we display ourselves as distinct personalities. Sometimes we are quite unaware of the impressions our actions and particularly the style and manner of our actions are creating. We may appear excitable, reserved, friendly, morose, strong-minded, stubborn; we may do things meticulously, slowly, carelessly, off-handedly, and so on. The front we present to particular people on particular kinds of occasions is our personality for them.

Character, on the other hand, is our reputation in the minds of others, particularly with respect to what one might call our moral qualities, such as integrity, slipperiness, reliability, propensity to gossip or intrigue. If our personality appears on the surface of our actions and in the expressive mode, our character is supposed to be a summary of the deepest and most stable features of our permanent inner selves. But it is gleaned from the experiences other people have of us, in social and other contacts, and is modified and transmuted in their gossip about us and their commentary upon our affairs. Attributions of character, then, are based upon much that appears as personality, but involve interpretation and moral assessment. Personality is shown, but character has to be read.

Empirical studies have shown that, contrary to traditional psychological theories, neither character nor personality are fixed and stable attributes of an individual human being (Argyle, 1976). Each varies according to the people with whom the person is interacting and the kinds of situations in which character and personality are displayed. A person may display fortitude (an attribute of character) in one kind of situation, and moral cowardice in another; on some occasions with some people he may be ebullient and outgoing, and on others gloomy and morose. Variability in the way a person presents himself to others is sometimes represented by distinguishing his 'personas' from his personality, where 'persona' is used for the way he appears to others on particular kinds of occasions, and 'personality' is reserved for the inner complex of cognitive resources a person needs to be able to be a skilled presenter of himself to others. He must be able to adopt the appropriate styles and expressive devices which are the conventions in his social milieux, for the public representation of himself as having this or that personality and character, by illustrating, for example, that he has this or that moral quality, such as fortitude. This could be done, for instance, by gritting the teeth, and expelling the breath in a long slow hiss.

The capacity to handle these changes in our public selves in a systematic fashion is one of the most important social skills. But we must also have a repertoire of personalities that lie within the acceptable bounds as defined in our society. We must neither pry too busily into the affairs of others nor be too uninterested, since we would probably wish to be considered neither a nosey-parker nor a recluse. We must be neither too obsessed with our own affairs nor too self-neglecting, since we would surely wish to be neither a show-off nor a doormat. Somehow we have to learn the boundaries of self-presentation.

Personality and character can be further distinguished in their relation to the time trajectory of our life courses. Character is popularly supposed to be immutable, and as the inner core of our being to be unaffected except by the most terrible or dramatic life events. Though personality is treated in everyday life as just as stable as character, and requiring something awful to change it, it is nevertheless also implicitly treated as undergoing growth and change. This can be easily seen in the way certain expressive styles are thought to be inappropriate to particular epochs in the life trajectory. A didactic style in the manner one uses to others may be quite acceptable and even expected in an elderly teacher but is quite unacceptable in a clever and well-read ten year old. Presenting oneself in the clothes and style of a playboy may be right and proper for a man of thirty but absurd and even pathetic in a man of sixty.

Names and the Management of Reality

The variability we have drawn attention to is certainly a marked feature of human interaction, but it is limited. The limitation arises not only from limits on the skill and social knowledge any individual may have, but from a person's physical and social endowments, such as his bodily shape and colour, his accent, manners and name. His given name may be something that he can wear with pride and utilise in his self-presentation. But it may be an attribute he does his best to conceal, since it may give away his social stigmas of various kinds.

But his nicknames, on the other hand, the names he has thrust upon him by his colleagues, playmates, friends and family, represent him as others see him. As we shall show, nicknames very often home in on just those characteristics he would prefer to forget. This is well understood by the victims. As one child put it, 'I dislike nicknames – people use them to imply your character. . .' Managing a nickname is one of the more fateful of social skills. Nicknames can serve not only as thumbnail character sketches, or illustrations of quirks of personality and physical appearance, but as capsule histories too, selecting and amplifying some moment in the life course that stands out as striking. Sometimes a name can stem from both: A.C.B., known as 'Muffy', offers the elision of 'Mumpsy', a name highlighting the awfulness of her appearance when she had the mumps, and 'Muffin', from Muffin the Mule, a tribute to her stubborness of character. Sometimes a nickname that derives from some internal manipulation of the language, for instance one based upon a rhyme, can suggest certain presentational possibilities which an active and reputation-seeking youngster can make the most of. For instance, Priscilla Brown decided Priscilla was too 'primish'. By manipulating the final syllables of her name she created and promulgated a nickname with a more lively ring. Priscilla yielded Cilla which became Calli(e). Though she reports that she is still prim Priscilla to her parents, she encourages the use of the matier Callie among her contemporaries and friends.

Anthropologists have noticed the tremendous importance some societies attach to naming. Levy-Bruhl in *Notebooks on Primitive Mentality* (1976) describes a tribe's method of detection in the case of theft.

> What matters to them is to have a mystic hold over the thief. They can then employ powerful means of magic to discover his name. If they are successful, then they have him and he will not escape them, for to primitives, the name serves not only to designate individuals. It is an integral part of the personality, it participates in it. If the name is discovered, the personality is mastered . . .

In our society, though we have no evidence that anyone subscribes to name magic in this sense, widespread beliefs in the power and fatefulness of names as social indicators, as devices to ensure psychological comfort in the presence of things and machines, shows up in the deep concern many parents have to find the right name for their child even before it is born, and the widespread use of names for cars, boats and so on. On the other hand, there is a kind of domestication of the exotic or the dangerous made possible by a particular kind of name. To call the Loch Ness Monster 'Nessie' goes some way to our coming to see it as tamed, as part of the familiar world of pets. There must be something of this too in the naming of hurricanes by the most ordinary of girl's names such as 'Bessie', 'Caroline' and so on, while battleships receive names like 'Indomitable' and 'Indefatigable'. It strikes us that not only are the meanings and associations of these names at work in the social definitions of these objects, as less and more threatening than they might be taken to be by nature, as it were, but there seems to be a phonetic appropriateness about them too. A cross-linguistic empirical study could perhaps be made to test the correctness of these intuitions.

The attempt to subdue things by naming them is beautifully illustrated by William Golding in *Pincher Martin*.

The book recounts the imaginary attempts of a drowning man to avert death at any cost. This he does by creating from his last few seconds of actual life an illusory six days cast away on a rock in the Atlantic. His struggles to sustain a belief in the illusion (and therefore a semblance of life) means he must continually assure himself of the reality of his fading life world.

On the third day of this imaginary existence, he names the various strange formations on the alien rock with names such as: 'Oxford Circus', 'Piccadilly', 'Leicester Square', 'The Red Lion', and then begins to deliberate aloud on his actions:

'I am busy surviving. I am netting down this rock with names and taming it. Some people would be incapable of understanding the importance of that. What is given a name is given a seal, a chain. If this rock tries to adapt me to its ways I will refuse and adapt it to mine. I will impose my routine on it, my geography. I will tie it down with names.'

Pincher uses names to give a tangible, rational meaning to his surroundings. A name used in this way functions as a point of personal reference, a method of categorising an environment and its events, into humanly comprehensible terms, by drawing upon the names for a familiar and, in a sense, domestic environment.

Names and Personality

Commonsense reflection on the influences that are likely to determine personality would suggest that a person's name and the various appellations which he acquires through life would be likely to have a considerable influence upon the kind of person he takes himself to be. A name would not perhaps be a *determining* feature of someone's personality, that is of the psychological basis of public versions of himself, but it seems reasonable to suppose that it is a basic datum to be managed by a person in his presentation system. In this respect it is a given, like one's physique and other physical characteristics, such as colour, facial form, and so on. Though names have an intransigent existence as objects determined by social practices outside an individual's control, such as, for example, christening and registering the name, their modification can lie within a person's sphere of influence since, at least in some countries, he is legally entitled to style himself anything he likes. Or, if his given name is sufficiently complex, he can choose which aspect of it to emphasise when he gives his name to other people. But given, official names are not the only names one acquires. They can also develop through the elaborate system by which other kinds of names are generated, acquired, managed, denied and so on, in the processes of the management of the social images of oneself. The obviousness of these reflections ought not to suggest that no further empirical work than mere social intuition is required. Our discussions in this book are based upon detailed investigations of naming practices in many parts of the world, and in many corners of society.

The investigation of the way in which a name is effective in influencing personality is a good example of a form of social psychological process which could not be understood by using the naive experimentalist approach. How could one proceed to test 'hypotheses' about the effect of names by manipulating the independent variable, in this case a person's name, and then seeing what effect it had? The impossibility of studying naming and its effects experimentally has perhaps been responsible for the almost complete absence from the literature of studies of the influence of names on the development of personality and social skill. For example, in neither Hollander and Hunt (1972) nor Secord and Backman (2nd edition, 1972) is naming as a determinant of personality discussed, nor are the roles of names and naming practices in social life anywhere mentioned. Surprisingly, the otherwise superb expose of the social world of schoolchildren by the Opies has only the scantiest discussion of nicknaming.

The first general observation to make is to draw attention to the peculiarly intimate sense in which one's name is oneself. This is illustrated in the familiar ambiguity of the question, 'Who are you?', which admits either of a name, 'James Callaghan', or a description of role or office, 'a prime minister', in answer. We believe, though we have not established this for certain, that the name usually has priority over the description. The fatefulness and consequentiality of the potency of giving one's name in answer is well enough illustrated by the uneasiness many people report when asked their names, and in more extreme cases by the feelings of shame, pride and so on clustering around a name which we will illustrate in several of the studies to be described. Very little empirical work has been done on the name emotions. By the nature of the case their study must be undertaken in a non-experimental style. The relationships between names and name emotions must be elicited in the accounts of people who have experienced them. We shall be exploring these matters in name autobiographies later in this book.

Anthropologists have investigated names and naming systems in much more detail than have psychologists. As we pointed out in the introduction, there are important studies of the systems and associated practices in which the 'real' name is concealed or actively looked for because of the control it is believed might be obtained over a person should an enemy obtain it.

The Genesis of Names

We shall be using an important anthropological distinction in the work which follows, namely that between internal and external influences on a naming system. Barley (1974) has called this the internal and external motivation in the giving of a name. Anthropologists have noticed that the choice of name is determined partly by systematic features of the naming system itself, as part of a language, and partly by empirical properties of the subject or individual named. For example in Barley's study this distinction allows him to explicate Anglo-Saxon royal naming practices as determined partly by an internal property of the names as words, namely their alliterative properties, choice being regulated by the Anglo-Saxon rules of poetic composition. These are needed to ensure the introduction of phonetic systematisation into sequences of names for mnemonic purposes. But name choice is also partly determined by external considerations, namely whether the person concerned is male or female. We shall find that the distinction between internal and external motivation in naming runs through most of the empirically gathered material upon which this book is based.

We shall distinguish throughout this study between given names, those that a person acquires through the official machinery of naming, and which in general he has little choice in deciding, and nicknames, the names he acquires informally, often contrary to his wishes. This is not a hard and fast distinction and we shall introduce other intermediate categories from time to time as they are required. There are some exceptions, too, to the general principle that given names are acquired rather than chosen. In some legal naming systems it is possible for a person to change his name officially and ceremonially to one of his own choice. It is also possible nowadays in English-speaking countries for a woman, on marriage, to choose to adopt her husband's name or to continue to be referred to by her maiden name. In the British system for the naming of persons raised to the peerage, the title taken by a man on elevation to that rank is a name of his own choice. Interestingly, this is not the case for women raised to the House of Lords. In general, though, we shall be justified in assuming that given names are acquired by an individual at, or shortly after, birth and that he or she has little say in what they will be.

By studying the widespread phenomenon amongst adolescents of wishing to change their names we have been able to get some idea of what names people would choose if they were able to do so. Commonsense understanding suggests that both names and nicknames are closely bound up with one's sense of identity. A disparity between actual and envisaged personality might appear as dissatisfaction with one's name. Such a disparity seems likely to become particularly prominent in the self-reflections of adolescence, and it could be managed by a shift of name in the direction of that taken to reflect a more desirable personality. This is indeed what we have found. We find much the same thing in the practice, still quite widespread, of the adoption of stage-names. For example, Norma Jeane Mortensen became 'Marilyn Monroe', and Jerry Dorsey became 'Engelbert Humperdinck'. Impresarios, who encourage such changes, must have some conception of what sort of name goes with what sort of personality. By tapping tacit understandings of the presentational force of names we get a grasp upon some of the ways names are thought to be fateful. One would expect these to be both culture-specific and changing over time. Investigations on a cross-cultural and historical basis might prove illuminating in revealing whether there are any universal principles that could be discerned in such cases, but we have had to leave that to other researchers, since our concern is with the social force of nicknaming systems in use amongst children and young people.

The Fatefulness of Names

To understand the social functioning of names it is important to grasp the fatefulness of many names, whether they be given names in the official sense of the name chosen for an individual by those held responsible for such matters and officially ratified and recorded, or nicknames. Because a name is not just a label or a mere neutral referential device, but is rich in content and many kinds of association, the effect of a name may last a lifetime. A very striking example of this is to be found in the account by Remedios Reyas in Fraser (1973) on the fatefulness of nicknames in a small Spanish town.

> The people are very witty. They invent nicknames in a flash. Everyone has one and they're often passed down from generation to generation. Usually people don't know the family by their real name but by the nickname. There are whole generations of Satans, Little Stars, Bad Feet. I imagine a woman looking at her new-born and saying, 'Ay, what a tiny prick he's got,' [so] the poor man has been 'Tiny prick' for the rest of his life.

To understand how the good and bad associations of names bear upon the development of self we need to know how and when one discovers one's names. One might assume, in the absence of empirical work, that knowledge of one's personal name and one's family name was acquired as social knowledge, that is from the way one was treated by other people, at different times in the course of one's development. This may or may not be so. There are various curious features about the early naming practices of parents to infants that we shall discuss in another section, summarising empirical work that has been done on that matter, which leads one to think that, at least in some cases, family name and personal name are both available to an infant at about the same age. Having discovered one's name, one then, bit by bit, we suppose, comes to understand its significance, quite apart from its role as an indexical and referential expression.

There must come a time at which some unfortunate children realise that their names are in themselves stigmas. There seem to be at least two possibilities for kinds of name stigma. Some names have, for a variety of reasons, become absurd, ridiculous, the object of derision. A recent example is the name stigma attached to 'Horace', which, so far as we can trace, seems to have had its origin in Walt Disney's use of the name for a particularly absurd horse. The popularity of the cartoon perhaps led to the rapid spread of that stigma. But there is another possibility which is now impossible to verify, namely that the name was already stigmatised and that Disney chose it for an absurd animal because it was an absurd name to him.

Again, there are traditional names which seem, as it were, intrinsically primed for joking and teasing. In Keith Waterhouse's story of a short period in the life of a boy who lived on the edge of a northern industrial town about twenty-five years ago, one anecdote has an autobiographical ring. It illustrates the stigmatising properties of the old Yorkshire surname 'Longbottom (botham).'

In the excerpt, the boy protagonist has just met a new and rather attractive neighbour:

> Told her my name. 'Anyway, what do they call *you*?' I said.
> 'Marion Longbottom.'
> Felt like saying: 'Why is your bottom long?' but I thought I'd better not, so I just said, 'Aw', instead.

The boy's chivalry, in steering away from the reflex taunting prompted by Marion's name, is set in direct contrast to the next incident. Marion and the boy have entered a den where they are obviously unwelcome. One of the first questions directed at Marion is:

> 'Do they call you Long bum?' Marion pretended not to hear.
> Barbara Monoghan and Kathleen Fawcett started whispering again.
> 'How old are you, Marion?' said Barbara.
> 'As old as my tongue and a bit older than my teeth,' chanted Marion.
> 'She's the same age as me, 'cos she's in our class,' said Kathleen Fawcett.
> 'Aren't you, Marion?'

'What if I am?'
'Oo, what if I am?' mimicked Barbara Monaghan, baring her teeth.

But name stigmas may be of other kinds. In those societies where there are stigmas attached to belonging to a particular race or religious community ethnically revealing names begin to acquire an emotional or attitudinal load in proportion to the stigma attached to the ethnicity. We shall be illustrating this form of stigmatisation and its management in the detailed studies in later chapters.

Stigmas are managed more or less successfully by the people who suffer them. Erving Goffman has made an extensive study of the systematic methods by which stigmas are managed. We owe to Johnny Cash an account of how stigmatic naming can be used by a parent to promote the development of character, cf. 'A boy called Sue'. The first step to management is related to an observation of Goffman's (1963).

Shame becomes a central possibility arising from the individual's perception of one of his own attributes as a defiling thing to possess and one he can readily see himself as not possessing. It is the poignancy of the person's realization that his name is something that might very well have been the other that makes name stigmas both so strikingly damaging and so apparently remediable.

In his general discussion Goffman identifies three different techniques by which stigmas can be managed.
1 It may be that those who cannot support a 'norm' by reason of their possession of a common stigma nevertheless become passionate supporters of that very norm. It is hard to see how this technique could be applied generally in the case of names, though it might have been an element in the anglicisation of names in nineteenth-century America.
2 A stigmatised individual may simply alienate himself from the community in which his peculiar name or other damaging personal characteristic would be stigmatising. We have not come across a social practice by which an adult manages a damaging name in such a way, either in our studies or in the literature. But we have reason to think that children do resort to this technique, though their efforts to break away are short-lived and often ineffective. Sometimes, though, they can start again by the drastic expedient of leaving a school where they have been particularly persecuted.
3 In so far as a person's name is implicated in generating the views others have of him, then change of name is itself a method of impression management. Changes may be subtle. Alterations in spelling can modulate a name from one ethnicity to another by change of apparent etymology, so for example, 'Rosenburg' becomes 'Montrose', or 'Battenburg' becomes 'Mountbatten'. Again, it is possible to shift

from one's given name to a more cosy diminutive, altering the projected personality, as for example the stiff 'Margaret' may give way to the matey 'Maggie'. One may even change one's name completely in adult life.

The management of nicknames is, of course, a much more difficult affair, since they are not so much within the personal power of the nicknamed as within the social practices of his peers. Most of our observations of techniques used to resist damaging nicknames involve either reprisals or reciprocal naming of an equally stigmatising character. Though it is not unreasonable to see unfortunate given names and denigrating nicknames as falling within the general category of stigmas as Goffman defines it, in the nature of the case they involve techniques of management which fall largely outside the methods Goffman recognises, since the strategy of concealment is not usually available. There are two exceptions to this that we have recorded. People generally try to conceal family or petnames from their peers unless they find them appropriate or otherwise engaging. So too, when passing from junior to secondary school most people leave their old nicknames behind, unless they pass up with a substantial body of old friends who can be relied upon to bring the nickname with them.

Complementary to the influence of name stigmas are the effects of the acquisition of names of which one might justly be proud. For example, one may have a name that connects one in some way with an honoured person, family, or ethnic group. However, the positive effects of names have, among some communities, not been simply left to chance. That is, parents have chosen virtue and good-quality names for their children. This was common practice in Victorian England, and it is presently still the custom amongst many Chinese families. An empirical investigation on the Chinese practices is presently being conducted to try to ascertain how far it is that Chinese parents who choose a virtue or quality name hope (and/or believe) that this will affect the character of their children. To add to this, an investigation of how far those who bear such names are able to identify in their psychological autobiographies any influences and occasions on which virtue followed a name has been conducted.

The fateful consequentiality of names depends upon the reading of one's own name or nickname by others, which is important only if there is a public understanding of the personality implications of this or that name. We have already pointed out that parental choice of names should reflect to some extent local understanding of these personality implications. The study of the Chinese and Japanese naming practices reveals some aspects of how other people's names are read. Similarly, the annual league tables of names published by the newspapers in England ought to reveal something of the social implications of certain names in the differential choices made in different parts of the country and in areas dominated by different kinds of professions and jobs. There do seem to be some pointers in this direction. The *Sunday Times* of 11 January 1976 reported a survey it had conducted in a somewhat jocular spirit, comparing four areas in Britain. There were distinct regional variations, which could perhaps be associated to some extent with class. There is a sharp difference between the degree to which Victorian girls' names are currently (1976) being used in the south and north of England, so that a name like Emma is found in the south more frequently than in the north. But class differences seemed much more potent than geographical distinctions in that, in an area where manual labour was the most common form of work, a somewhat more elaborate form of naming was apparent and the names seemed to have been influenced to some extent by American naming practices, whereas, in those areas of London where the predominantly professional workers live, the standard, traditional and simple names predominated. A further complication, which runs counter to the simple-versus-elaborated names, is to be found by a recent trend to classical, i.e. Greek and Roman, names, particularly for girls, as for example 'Olympian', the name of Alexander's mother.

Such work as reported in newspapers is, of course, rudimentary. What lies behind it is a hitherto unexplored feature of tacit social knowledge, namely, the social and personality associations of names. This is the kind of thing which 'everybody knows', but which until recently has not been systematically explored. There is, for example, a kind of parlour game played in some families, involving guessing the sort of person who is likely to be the bearer of a particular kind of name. Sometimes this turns out to be an idiosyncratic product of meeting this or that person who had the name.

The social aspects of given names, then, seem, from our common-sense intuitions and unreflective experience, to be associated in various ways with matters of personalities, that is, with the self as presented to others, with the public version of oneself. It is also clear that a considerable amount of empirical work must be done to extend our knowledge of this hitherto unconsidered matter.

The Special Interest of Nicknames

The richest and also the most obvious place to start systematic research on the relation of names to the development of personality and social competence is in the autonomous social world that children construct independently of adult influences, a world which exists outside the classroom and away from the places where adult conceptions of sociality reign. It is in this autonomous world that the nickname has a special place. A large proportion of this book is devoted to the study of the social and psychological power of nicknames, as opposed to names of any other sort. Perhaps, therefore, we should pause to justify this singularity.

The reason for singling out nicknames for special attention may be put as follows:

1 The nicknaming systems which have their origins in small groups and which, as we shall see, play such an important part in their social organisation, offer the sociologist and social psychologist a rare chance to examine the system of relationships which occur when children construct a social order for themselves.

2 The field of nicknaming is again a rare example of children using language creatively in accordance with a logic which is not laid down from outside. Our first task will be to discover what that logic is.

Why is it important, one might ask, to look for relationships between nicknames and what might be called 'social competence', the ability a person has to interact smoothly with other people in the management of the activities of his world and particularly in the development of personal reputation and character, and the social effects of domination and subordination that flow from it? There are particular reasons why the results of this sort of study could be valuable, for example, to teachers, parents, and anyone else with the management of children and with the growth and development of their personalities.

1 A teacher usually sees his pupils when he is in a position to 'define the situation', when he and the classroom or other socially loaded surroundings dominate each encounter. However, the welcome his teaching receives will certainly be influenced by the micro-social world the children have constructed, if not actually be determined by it. Hargreaves (1967) has pointed out the important effects of the attitudes of the cliques that form in the child's world on the attitude to learning. We shall be contending that nicknames and the social practices in which they play an essential role are an important part of this secret world and deserve attention for that reason alone.

2 The opportunities to relate to society begin from birth, but the school offers for most children the first experience of a society larger than the family and one where the particular individual is not automatically the centre of attention and, in most families, loving care. The way a child deals with other people at this formative period will colour very strongly the way in which relationships are formed in adult life, we believe, but the final establishment of that idea will require a return to the people we have studied and the data we have accumulated when many years have passed. This we propose to do. Our present project is part of this overall interest. Since nicknames, we have shown, are an important part of the control mechanism of childhood society, their management, it is therefore not unreasonable to suppose, should have important social consequences later on.

A simple-minded idea of what it is to carry on a scientific study is sometimes allowed to distort the range of methods available to a social investigator. In particular, it is sometimes supposed that the objectivity of science is to be achieved by keeping the observed and the observer as far apart as possible. However, this approach is neither desirable nor even attainable if it were. Up to a point our method involves statistical measures and graphical techniques, but, even in collecting the data upon which these methods operate, the participants' own reactions, emotional attitudes and so on must be incorporated. This is the method of ethogenics and we believe it to be particularly appropriate to this study, since we are concerned with the way in which people fit themselves into a society, partly, but not wholly, of their own creation. In this context, a 'subjective' approach is positively required by the canons of scientific method, and is not merely a scientific second-best forced on us by the nature of the material and processes we are studying. Nicknames encapsulate the way bearers are perceived by others in their social worlds, and at the same time serve as public representations of the locally valid ideas about what way an acceptable person is supposed to be.

But before we begin our survey it is important to be clear about which appellations should count as nicknames. In this context it is helpful to bear in mind the etymology of the term. A nickname is an *eke-name*, derived from the Old English verb *ecan*, meaning 'to add to or augment'. Thus an eke-name was a name given to a person over and above his legal or baptismal name. In practical terms this means that simple abbreviations of officially given names such as 'Dave' or 'Chris' will not count as nicknames, although the use of such forms may have great significance in certain contexts. But since they add to or augment the names we already have, a detailed study of extra names must be founded upon a thorough grasp of the ways official names are given and of the attitudes that people may come to have towards them.

2
Choosing a Name

Choosing a Name for a Child

Many peoples seem to have believed that a causal or some more generalised influence obtains between a person's name and his character, personality and even his fate. There is evidence of a widespread belief that a name represents or even encapsulates the very being of an individual creature, whether corporeal or spiritual. To be a successful exorcist one had first to find out the names of the devils infesting a victim, since they would leave only if conjured in terms of their proper names.

In the light of these ideas about the influence and power of names it is not surprising that the naming of an infant should be a matter of concern. Much of non-European practice and belief is summed up in this quotation from von Hagen (1973):

As soon as the woman was pregnant, she was put under the protection of the god Tezcatlipoca. There is a pictured history in the *Codex Mendoza* of the birth, naming, rearing, discipline of a child, of the details of swaddling and the type of cradle. When the child was born, a magician was brought in by the parents from their own local clan temple. He consulted a horoscope, a sort of book of fate, which was unrolled to its twenty-foot length. This was to determine if the child had been born under good or bad auguries. The naming was important, and if they found that the day was unlucky, the naming was put off till a better moment—the avoidance of misfortune itself is the enjoyment of positive good. 'What's in a name?' To the Indians, everything. Many primitives have two names, social and personal. The personal was known and used only by the immediate family in the belief that if used too often, it might lose its power. In times of illness, the witch doctor used the real name to call the dying back to life. Boys were called after their fathers or grandfathers, usually dynamic names, such as 'Smoking Crest' (*Chimalpopoca*), 'Obsidian Serpent' (*Itzcoatl*), 'Speaking Eagle' (*Quauhtatoa*); girls, who seem always to evoke a sense of poetry, were named after flowers, stars, birds, as 'Ibis' (*Atototl*), 'Green Flower' (*Matlal-xochitl*), or 'Rain Flower' (*Quiauh-xochitl*).

Cultural Stereotypes

Despite the disappearance from our culture of such beliefs and the conventions that go with them (instanced by the decline both in the use and the seriousness of the saint's names as given names in Northern Europe, though the practice persists in Spain), it seems reasonable to suppose that individual people still associate certain personal characteristics with a name. We have been able to confirm this not only in England but in Spain. One would expect such associations on the grounds that in coming across someone of unusual or striking character and appearance these personal characteristics would be thought of when the name cropped up, even in the absence of traditions concerning the power of names and their influence on character and fate. Similarly there might be long-standing associations of a certain range of names with occupations, social and/or economic classes and so on, as there are more obviously with race and gender.

A simple non-human example of the specificity of names is found in the naming of pets. Dogs tend still to run to the traditional dog-names such as Rover. Hounds answer to such names as Rex, Rover, Butch, while cats get names like Tibbles, Tabby, Whiskers. Even inventive name-giving recognises specific differences. A traveller reports that a large, black, bad-tempered Great Dane, resident in a small Spanish town, is called 'Dog', while a well-known Oxford domestic cat is nicknamed 'Le Shah (Chat) d'Iffley'.

Many of the associations between names and personal characteristics must surely be idiosyncratic and accidental. We have not considered these worth exploring in this study, though they would be an important element in an idiographic, intensively designed study of the psychology of individual people, since some of an individual's attitudes to others might be shaped by such contingencies.

However, we believe that it is reasonable to suppose that some names do acquire a wider stereotypical significance. We know that some proper names can become so strongly associated with the qualities of their most prominent bearer that they are transformed into adjectives, as for example, 'Churchill' gives rise to 'churchillean' and 'Napoleon' to 'napoleonic'. In exploring the reasons for parental name choice and the effect that bearing a particular name has upon someone's life, we must find out whether indeed there are any noticeable associations with specific names that are less obvious than those of the names of the famous and infamous, and yet are not wholly idiosyncratic.

To this end we asked people to contemplate ten fairly common men's and ten fairly common women's names, and to jot down in a few words any personal characteristics they would expect a person bearing such a name to have. The results were striking. (For those who believe in such things, we remark that results reported as positive in this study are significant to the 0·05 level or better.)

Among the men's names, 'Eric', 'Paul', 'Michael' and 'Claud', had only idiosyncratic associations. 'Austin', and 'James' showed some generality, though too weak to place much credence in. But the bearers of some names were expected to have strongly marked characteristics.

Christopher	is expected to be fair-haired, tall and charming
Nicholas	is expected to be pleasant
Matthew	is expected to be quiet and studious

Among women's names, 'Doreen', 'Sarah', 'Emma', 'Jane' and 'Jo' seemed to have only idiosyncratic associations. For the rest,

Gloria	is expected to be blonde and outgoing
Mary	is expected to be gentle
Alexandra	is expected to be 'superior'
Billie	is expected to be a tom-boy
Elsie	is expected to be motherly

These conclusions are drawn from a study of the name associations of adults. A parallel study among thirteen-year-old girls shows that they seem to share the stereotypes of adults, for the most part. 'Christopher' is fair and kindly, 'James' markedly upper class, 'Lee' is a trouble-maker and 'Paul' is tall, dark and handsome. 'Gloria' is blonde and jolly, 'Elsie' is old, plump and a good sort, 'Emma' is pretty and 'Jane' is plain. (We owe these last results to Sarah Davis.)

In our next study we asked people to choose an appropriate name for a person whose appearance and character we sketched in briefly. The results were quite striking. (Significant results in these and the following surveys were found with English-speakers of native English birth and upbringing. Celts and Americans do not seem to share these stereotypes. We have no doubt that a wider survey would show they have their own.) Of the six thumbnail sketches of men, four were named at random, but two showed a strong effect. A man who was described as 'fair, short, plump, jolly and not too bright' was frequently called 'Fred', while another described as 'bald, ruddy complexion, beery, cheerful but with sour undertones' was regularly called 'George'.

For women the effect was even more marked. There was no doubt that a woman who was 'blonde, motherly and fairly cheerful' was called

'Gloria', that someone 'dark, well-built, forceful, glasses, trouser-suited' was called 'Margaret', that someone 'blonde, small, pale and tearful' was called 'Jane', and someone 'tall, willowy, fair, slow of speech and with an upper-class accent' was called either 'Elizabeth' or 'Penelope'.

But we have little or no evidence that suggests that such stereotypes have much influence on how parents come to choose a name for their child. Once someone does have such a name the stereotype does seem to have some effect on what the child has to do to cope with the problems of living with the name, since in name-teasing the stereotype provides the initial ammunition.

Simple liking and disliking of names may have more to do with parental choice, so our next step was to explore how far certain names are liked or disliked (in 1977). Again, the results of our survey were quite striking.

Of all the boys' names offered to our participants, 'James' stands out as very widely liked, while 'Christopher', 'Matthew' and 'Paul' are also popular. On the other hand, 'Edgar' is widely disliked, while 'Bert', 'Willy', 'Theodore', 'Fred' and 'Claud' are about equally unpopular. At first glance the unpopular names seem to be rather an odd collection, but a little closer look suggests an interpretation which we have not so far taken back to our participants to check. 'Edgar', 'Theodore' and 'Claud' strike us as both stereotypical and old-fashioned upper-class names, while 'Fred', 'Bert' and 'Willy' have much the same period flavour among lower class names. It looks as if the obloquy into which they have fallen reflects a rejection of both extremes of the social spectrum.

Girls' names show a somewhat different profile. 'Doreen', 'Elsie', 'Phyllis' and 'Billie' are widely disliked, while 'Emma', 'Sarah', 'Felicity', 'Penelope' and 'Laura' are widely liked. The former strike us as both stereotypical and old-fashioned lower-class names, while among the latter 'Sarah' and 'Felicity' seem to us plainly upper class.

Parental choice

Interestingly the results of the survey concerned with the simple matter of whether a name is liked or disliked are not reflected in the statistics of actual name giving. Names like 'John' and 'Elizabeth', though always high in the statistics, are only moderately liked. This suggests that other criteria are at work in actual choice of names. For example, an analysis of accounts of how a name was selected show, for example, that 'Elizabeth' was chosen as a name both because it is widely used throughout Europe, and because it offers considerable opportunity for modification by its bearer, since it is capable of a wide range of socially differentiated diminutives, ranging from the flamboyant 'Lizzie' to the stolid 'Beth'. To resolve this apparent paradox we turn to a detailed study of how parents choose a name for a child.

Our procedure took the usual ethogenic form. A questionnaire was compiled expressing our rough guesses as to the considerations parents weighed in making their choice. The way this was answered led to a systematic collection of accounts in subsequent discussions with them.

The forms so compiled asked for the christian or given name and then for the reasons for the choice. A variety of possible grounds were suggested: that the sound of the name had been a criterion, that a desire to perpetuate a family name contributed to the making of a certain choice, that a famous person's name had provided the inspiration, or that the name was evocative of type of person favoured by the parents as a model. A large and, we hope, inviting space was left for people's own comments, ideas and opinions. With reference to the suggestions we had provided the following distribution appears.

Sound	*Family*	*Famous person*	*Model*	*Other*
40%	38%	10%	10%	2%

This does, however, oversimplify results that were remarkable for their diversity and variety. In their own accounts people provided an insight into some unexpected factors in name choice, such as the construction of a name by making an anagram of parental names or, more poignantly, the choice of a name as part of an attempt at parental reconciliation. Less surprising was the influence of forceful family members in determining the parents' choice. A few clear trends and general concerns were very much apparent, however.

The given name was rarely considered alone*, but usually seen in the context of its juxtaposition to the surname. Indeed, permutations were painstakingly worked out with relation to the surname. 'Robert Andrew Morgan' for instance, was abandoned because of the embarrassing word formed from the initials. 'Ram' was thought to be too overtly sexual in implication. One mother gave up 'Matthew' for her new baby boy with some reluctance. Matthew Mortimer, she reasoned, would have the same initials as Mickey Mouse. So she abandoned 'Matthew' for 'David'.

Conversely, other parents took an obvious delight in fully exploiting the mutual impact of both names with a deliberate word play. Mr and Mrs Hills decided to make their rather ordinary name slightly more memorable by calling their daughter 'Beverley'. But their efforts were overshadowed by the parents Mr and Mrs Ray who called their daughter 'Sunshine'. Clearly, some parents go to extreme lengths to avoid associations that others welcome. But whichever way they react surnames are an important consideration to them.

*A number of parents report studying the etymology of proposed names, looking for 'good' meanings. Such books as Partridge (1959) *Name This Child* and Woulfe (1923) *Irish Names for Children* are widely consulted.

The traditional abbreviations of first names again divide parents into those that react positively and those that react negatively. One mother determined that the names she chose for her children should not be capable of contraction, so she named the first three 'Ann', 'Frank' and 'Kay'. But by the time the fourth was born 'Ann' had been *expanded* to 'Annie', 'Frank' was called 'Frances' by his teachers, and Kay's schoolfriends always wanted to know what 'Kay' was short for, perhaps 'Kathryn'? If names cannot be abbreviated it seems necessary to lengthen them. The fourth child in this family was called 'Gillian' in a quite devil-may-care proliferation of syllables and has been called 'Jill' from birth. There seems to be a tendency, whose source we are quite unable to locate, even after our extensive studies, to mess about with names. The example shows that parents who try to avoid this by choosing an abbreviated form as the official name are likely to find it expanded. Still, many do prefer abbreviations and we have records of people who ask for 'Kate' rather than 'Kathryn', 'Penny' instead of 'Penelope', or 'Hettie' for 'Harriet'.

The birth of a child can often be seen by parents as the beginning of a new generation and thus of a mini-dynasty. This suggests using the choice of name to strengthen a link with the family heritage by choosing or initiating a family name. The most striking example where we can surely infer the influence of this factor can be seen in the names of alternate generations of an established family. The Churchills have alternated 'Winston' and 'Randolph' in successive generations for a considerable time. Such practices provide models for those of less ancient lineage.

The influence of previous generations may not be so prevalent or so important in the choice of names for most families whose sense of continuity does not usually extend for more than three generations, but it is nevertheless a surprisingly common one. Thirty-eight per cent cited it as a consideration when naming a child. One mother, having chosen 'Carine' and 'Stuart' for her children gave as her reasons that 'Carine' was chosen to represent her own French extraction, while 'Stuart' reflected her husband's Scottish descent. More specific connections are established by christening a child after a recently dead member of the family. We record an Emma Jane who derived her second name as a result of the death of a great aunt, and a Theresa Grace who was born on the day her Aunt Grace died. Frequently the second, if not the first, given name of a child will perpetuate its descent. This principle is still in systematic use in Scotland. A survey of names on the examination papers of women undergraduates at a Scottish university showed that nearly all had their mother's surname as a second given name.

In the seventeenth century and later, infants were given such names as 'Faith', 'Hope' and 'Charity' by their Puritan parents, presumably in the hope that the offspring would embody this or that particular virtue when they matured. Religious tradition, especially the Catholic tradition, still influences naming through the choice of saints' names as given names. But the once powerful influence of St Mary, St Cecilia and so on, as name models, is noticeably diminishing today. However, the emulation idea still continues in more informal ways. The idea that a child should grow up towards a standard implied by his name has not disappeared. The standards are no longer represented by the words for abstract virtues or the names of saints. They have been replaced by pop-stars and TV characters and personalities as exemplars. Our studies strongly suggest that such people now have a similar status in many people's eyes as did the traditional saints and monarchs. The child is named accordingly. We are convinced from the study of parental accounts that local patriotism is not enough to explain the extraordinary case of the football supporter who named his son after the entire Everton team. 'John', 'Paul', 'George' and even 'Ringo' appeared in the mid-1960s as chosen because of the Beatles, though the first three names are reasonably common and 'John' the commonest of all. They displaced the 'Clark', 'Gary' and 'Marilyn' of an earlier period. But we should emphasise that the choice of a name according to an exemplar is found in only 10 per cent of cases.

Films do still exercise some influence. We have a record of a child called 'Lee', now seven years old. He was born during the time that the film *Paint Your Wagon* was in vogue. Lee's parents had seen and enjoyed the film and now say that they chose the name because it suggested to them the name of the star, Lee Marvin. They cannot remember anyone else they knew or knew of in their home neighbourhood being called by this name before they decided on it for their child.

But ideal-types are sometimes drawn from the family circle. For example, a couple report that they had first thought of the name 'John', because it sounded a good, honest name. But further discussion disclosed that it also had ideal-type properties through family connections. The father had had an uncle named 'John' who had run off to join the navy at the outbreak of the First World War and was killed at the early age of seventeen. He was a person that the father would have liked to meet, and who in the father's eyes had shown exemplary patriotism and devotion to duty.

A group of a similar size to those christened by reference to an individual as an example, are those whose name was chosen because it evokes a type. The continuing association of a name with an era, as well as personal associations with a personality type mean that the linked names become a general referent for that age or the particular characters and personalities associated with it. Mothers, especially, cited as the reasons for choosing such names as 'Emma', 'Louise' and 'Charlotte', simply that since these were old-fashioned and gentile they reminded them of a crinoline and old-lace past, but one whose agreeable associations were not forgotten. Henry John, though only two days old, was thus christened in the hope that in a few years' time he would be displaying those Victorian attributes of sterling worth and manly character that his parents admired. About 10 per cent of parents with whom we discussed these matters had christened their child with a name that brought back memories or evoked associations with a treasured past.

Much, as might be expected, depends on idiosyncratic or chance associations. For example, we have the case of the father who wanted to call his daughter 'Wendy' because he had known the brother of Sir James Barrie, the author of *Peter Pan*, the play in which Wendy is a prominent character. Interestingly, in this case the mother insisted that 'Wendy' should be the child's middle name, in case she grew up too tall for it. There might have been more to this negotiation, since as the result of a small empirical survey we were able to show that Wendy is a name disliked by women but liked by men. The child discussed above, now grown up, reports on reactions to her name which support our survey.

> 'I've always pulled faces about the name "Wendy". My mother
> thought that "Wendy" might be a silly name if my build turned
> out to be not exactly fairy-like. I'm glad she got her way. Any girls
> who find out that my middle name is "Wendy" have a good snigger
> at it, but any men who come across my name think it's lovely,
> and even prefer it to "Patricia" — which just goes to show you can't
> please everybody...'

Chance coincidences, too, play a role. As an example a respondent tells us that in the couple of days preceding his birth while his mother was already in the maternity hospital, the name 'Christopher' 'came to her out of the blue'. On reflection she now claims that this association was prompted by the proximity of Christmas, our respondent having been born on 8 December, and by the fact that his grandmother was called 'Christina'.

A nice example, combining both linguistic (internal) and associative (external) motivations appears in *Joby*, by Stan Barstow (1973). Joby's best friend, Snap, comes to call, but since Joby's mother is going to hospital that very day he leaves disappointed. This conversation follows:

> ' "Snap",' Joby's mother said, 'wherever did he pick up a name
> like that?'
> 'It's his initials. Sidney, Norman, Arthur, Prendergast. S.N.A.P.
> See?'
> 'Sidney, Norman Arthur ... Well, that's a right mouthful, an' no
> mistake. Nearly comes up t'Royal Family. I make no wonder he's

a bit dozy with a stringful of names like that hanging around his neck.'
'Snap's not dozy. He's got lots o' brains.'

Whether parents are for or against abbreviations, whether in favour or disapproving of intersecting combinations with surnames, whether continuing a family name, commemorating a loved one, emulating a notable person or identifying with a general type, one factor played a major role in all name choices. A name had to *sound* right. However strong the influence of these other factors if the name sounded wrong considered in combination with surname or even when the parents looked at the child, it was *never* given. No general principles of euphony have emerged however. 'Stuart', 'Gareth', 'Cedric', 'Felicity', 'Maggie', and 'Joan' were some of the phonetically very diverse names chosen, according to parents, simply because they appealed to the ear. Occasionally a simple, even naive, principle is clearly at work. We report without comment 'Roland Bolan' and 'Zowie Bowie'. In short, the aural impact was usually the deciding factor in name choice, dominant after all other influences had left their mark.

Case History : 'Carl' and 'Emma' : A Mother's Account

To give the flavour of parental cogitations we offer this unedited, first-hand account.

'Names you chose for your children originate very largely, I think, from knowing other endearing children who appear to suit their names very well. Such was the case with our choosing "Emma" as a prospective name if we were "blessed" with a daughter. Last year during the summer we stayed in a caravan. Our neighbours were a family from Birmingham who had two daughters. The name of the eldest eludes me (she was quite non-descript, obviously!) but the younger was monkey-faced little elfin Emma, who had the most original little mannerisms (—one of which was wetting her knickers) so Mike and I fell in love with her and so agreed that the name "Emma" would be ideal if we had a little girl.

'I certainly don't think that we gleaned the name from television, or any of the other media, and this applies to the boy's name that we considered—"Carl".

' "Carl" has always appealed to me because of a handsome young man of that name with whom I used to associate in my youth. Mike has no special brain waves as to why he too has always liked the name "Carl", other than a teenage rival of that name who was madly good looking and who "got the girls".

'Another thing strikes me about the name Emma. When I was at school I remember a teacher reading us a story, although I've long since forgotten title and author. It was all about a little girl who got locked in a coal-cellar. I remember one particular line in the story quite distinctly, where she shouts ". . .Emmy in de coal 'ole" . . . I suspect that this is short for Emily rather than Emma, but since then it has always struck me as a lovable and feminine name.'

Dissatisfaction with One's Name

We can get an indirect look at the kinds of considerations that make a name 'good' by a brief study of what makes a name 'bad'. We have collected some typical reasons for being dissatisfied with a name, with a sample of names that people would like to have instead. Ready-made examples can be found in show business. Why did Harry Webb become 'Cliff Richard' and Priscilla White change her name to 'Cilla Black'? Since this study is concerned with the use of nicknames, particularly in childhood and adolescence, we have not undertaken a detailed study of the criteria employed in the theatre and pop-music circles. We do know that the present Mr Matt Munro chose his name in a discussion with friends not for its sound, but for the way it would look when printed in an advertisement or set up outside a theatre.

This example suggests that there is probably much in the criteria that depends upon the physical properties of names as words in determining whether they are liked or not. We have already noticed the great stress parents put upon a name sounding right, so it is no surprise to find that in the theatre the look of name would be an important consideration. In a way adult decisions of this kind involve quite practical considerations. But do children, when they are dissatisfied with their names, advert to the same features? Sensitivity to the effect one's name might have on one's fellows does, indeed, extend beyond the footlights. Of the sample of young people we have examined, about a third have at some time or another wished that the names their parents had given them had been different. For example, some typical comments run as follows:

'I don't like my Christian name "Jonathan" being shortened to "Johnny". I like the idea of "Pythagoras".'
'Yes, I have thought of changing my name. I'd like a slicker name than Richard, i.e. "Dan Druff" or "Dee Generate". I don't like being called "Richard" or something "official".'
'I'd like to change my name from "Charles" to "Andrew".'
'I wanted to be called "David" instead of "Miles".'
'I don't mind most of my names—but I'd like to change my middle name "Julian".'

'My initials are T.A.T.—which signifies a certain part of the male anatomy not present among the Jewish community—I just want a total eradication of the said anatomical name.'

'My sister hates her name "Hilary". She says it sounds "fat".'

'I didn't like being called "Julia" after I realised that when some people called "Ju" it made some anti-semitic people think I was Jewish and dislike me.'

The Case of 'Mike'

Michael reports that he disapproved of his name being shortened to 'Mike'. His reasons were tortuous. He had gone up to university to read Oriental Studies, specialising in Near Eastern languages, Hebrew, Aramaic and Syriac. So he knew that the name 'Michael' is Hebrew in origin and means 'Who is like God' (מִכָּאֵל). The syllable 'el' (אֵל) at the end of the name translates into English as 'God'. Michael intended to enter the priesthood. Consequently, he objected to being called 'Mike', 'since it left the "God-bit" off'. The range and diversity of these informally collected comments suggested that a systematic survey should be undertaken. This revealed that there were indeed a few trends.

1 The majority of changes that were suggested were in christian names only. Most seemed to accept their surnames without question, even if given the opportunity to express an opinion. One person did say that he wanted to change his surname 'because it is prominent'.

2 There are definite (and perhaps rather predictable) trends in the sort of names that people would rather be without. Among those names that their owners believe they would be well rid of are:

Julian	Richard
Miles	Andrew
Samuel	Anthony
Callister	Augustus
Thomas	Charles
Tyrer	John

Whilst not all of these names are particularly out of the ordinary, taken as a whole the image they present at first hearing is perhaps a little exclusive, and probably not just a little effete. Rather surprisingly, the relatively inoffensive name 'Richard' seemed almost universally unpopular. Whether this is a national trend or not will presumably show up in the *Times*'s names survey in about ten years' time.

3 It is not so easy to make generalisations in terms of *preferences* for substitute names. If the people in the survey were not totally satisfied with their present names, then neither were they always very clear

about what positive changes they would like to make. Nevertheless, there are some definite preferences:

Jonathan	Mark
David	Stephen
Paul	Ian
Simon	

'Jonathan' and 'David' were far more popular names than any of the others put together. 'David' and 'Jonathan' have appeared together as favourites in the Old Testament. Curiously enough, with the exception of 'Ian', all the favoured names are biblical. This seems to link the preferences among adolescents in England quite strongly with the adult preferences reported already. A name with a long history has probably appeared in all sorts of social milieux, so that specific associations are continuously deleted. Although the deletion theory seems the most plausible, we are unable to offer any specific evidence in favour of it.

The most marked case we have recorded involves three brothers, Allan, David and James. The eldest and youngest are conspicuously clever, while David is perhaps only moderately bright. When Allan got a scholarship to Oxford, David saved up his pocket money till he had enough money to pay for changing his middle name to 'Allan' by deed-poll. So far as we know, Allan and David were not particularly close. In the absence of accounts we can only guess at the strength of background feeling and the nature of the thinking involved in this. It could involve anything from deviation to respect. It might be a case of an attempt to use sympathetic magic.

Just as adolescents express dissatisfaction with the names their parents gave them, so they sometimes dislike and resent their nicknames. A smallish boy found that one of the leaders of fashion in his school form gave him the nickname 'Halo' because he never seemed to do anything wrong. After a while Halo decided that he was not particularly enamoured of this new name so he set about ridding himself of it. Another person in the group assured us that Halo had succeeded in this ambitious project; whenever anyone called him by the name he acted 'hard', i.e. he began to call the person who had started calling him 'Halo' by the name 'Ruby', which apparently derived from the appearance of his antagonist's lips. This name stuck, so his opponent tried to rid himself of it by dropping the name 'Halo' for his tormentor. This example illustrates a very common pattern of social interaction, namely, reciprocal name-calling. We shall see this put to work in a number of contexts.

As we have shown, there are some given names that people would prefer to be called. And we find that the same is true of nicknames. Sometimes a person can achieve a nickname for himself. In the course of our studies in Spain we came across a boy whose parents had given him the name 'Daniel' but who had managed to go by a name of his own choice when with his classmates. The name he wanted was 'Niki'. He informed us of this ambition before he knew of our interest in nicknames. He wrote explaining the reason for his choice, 'Because I like Formula One motor racing and my favourite driver was Jackie Stewart, but he retired. And now my favourite is Nicky Lauder so my "apodo" is "Niki".' (*Apodo* is the Spanish word for nickname.) How was it possible for him to achieve such a name? His social position in the form was high. He appeared in the top half of the 'pecking order' and belonged in the most dominant of the three cliques which comprised it. This emerges clearly in a sociogram of the interaction and dominance structure of the relevant cliques.

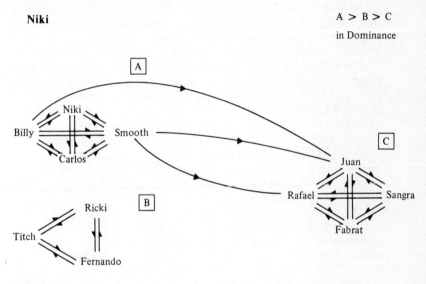

Figure 1

Some further evidence on dissatisfaction with one's given name comes from a large-scale study by Busse and Helfrich (1975) made in the United States. They found that there were differential ratings of names amongst both boys and girls. Unfortunately they have not published an analysis of which names were liked and which disliked. But they have found that there are changes in the ratings girls make of girls' names as they get older, there being a particularly sharp change from 'pre-teen' to 'teenager'. There are much smaller changes in girls' rating of boys' names, and in boys' ratings generally. Here they do tell us a little about the actual names, noting that 'short, traditional girls' names (e.g. Linda, Nancy, etc.) are replaced as favourites by longer, more "modern" ones (e.g. Christine, Jennifer).' Busse and Helfrich explain their findings by the idea that girls are more conscious of themselves and their public persona, and consequently are more inclined to criticise their names as representations of their public image, so to speak. They make the intriguing observation that it was largely girls who took up the fad of changing the spellings of their first names, though they do not follow this up or tell us any detail. Other American material can be found in Finch *et al.* (1944), Rossi (1965), Cumming (1967) and Hartmann *et al.* (1968).

3
Petnames

The very first 'eke-names' that a child comes into contact with are the names invented for him by the very parents who so painstakingly worked out what to call him for the registrar of births, deaths and marriages. We shall distinguish names of this sort, invented by parents for very young children, as 'petnames', reserving the name 'nickname' for those 'eke-names' which are invented mostly by a child's own companions and classmates, a prisoner's cellmates, and so on. We notice in passing that lovers and intimate friends often construct names for each other having something of the quality of petnames and with a similar etymology. Disapproval of or anger with the other can lead to a retreat from petname to formal name. This happens routinely in families, as well as in those groups where petnames mark adult relations of intimacy and affection. One of the authors recollects being told that torturers sometimes have petnames for some of their victims, though we have been unable to verify the reference.

The importance of the study of petnames derives for us from their place as possible precursors of nicknames. An obvious problem raised by the existence of nicknames is how a child acquires the capacity to recognise that there is more than one nominative device being used to refer to him. How early, one might ask, is the idea that a person can have more than one name acquired by him? According to our studies the capacity to be able to take oneself as the referent of several appellations must develop very early in a child's life. So far as we have been able to discover, it is routine practice, throughout the human community, for each parent, in cultures as diverse as Britain, Mexico and Japan, to use as many as nine distinct names for their infant, before he is yet one year old. Taking both parents together, they may be using as many as twelve distinct names for a child of six months. From the accounts we have of the use of multiple petnames, children at that early age seem quite capable of grasping that they are the referent of all of them. The capacity to respond to sequentially acquired sets of names looks as if it is developed very early. We present this feat as a problem. Developmental psychologists might well study the genesis of this capacity.

Nothing is yet known about how an infant acquires the ability to receive the name as his and, in particular, as a young child, to receive from parents, friends, siblings and others, his first nicknames. Empirical studies have shown that, seemingly independent of particular culture, an infant is bombarded with a variety of names, none of which is his official name, and any one of which may be used by his parent, or parents, to refer to him. He seems to know how to cope with this multiplicity of referring expressions long before he can talk. The names employed by husband and wife for an infant are systematically different with a certain overlap. Each may use anywhere between five and eight names for the child and to the child, none of which is the name they chose for purposes of official registration, though some of these names are, of course, related to it; one example of such official name-related cognomen being a contraction as, for example, 'Benjamin' becoming 'Benjos'. Similarly, there seems to be a practice for fathers to use a very formal mode of address as a mark of affectionate intimacy, referring to their daughters as 'Miss So-and-So' and sons as 'Mr So-and-So', or whatever might be the appropriate formal title. Work done so far has found no evidence of this practice by mothers. Finally, there is a use of descriptive phrases like, 'Baby man', or *'Nane'*, that is a referential term which has the force of a nickname. Much more work requires to be done to understand this practice more thoroughly, but it has two striking characteristics.

1 The child is subjected to a multiplicity of referring expressions and seems to be capable of realising that it is he or she that is meant by whichever name they happen to be addressed.

2 There is a difference in the naming practices of mothers and fathers, each using a multiplicity of names, but drawing on slightly different lists.

For instance, an English couple use seven distinct nominative expressions in common for an infant girl christened 'Victoria', but only the father uses the curious name 'Tontees'. He cannot recall its origins, even though the child is less than a year old. It is quite certainly not derived from the child's own ineffectual efforts to pronounce its own name, since it is as yet too young to make them. A Mexican couple, parents of a male infant Juan Jesús, rarely use the child's official name, but have four petnames in common. However, each parent has to hand three other names which only he or she uses. And they are very different. The mother uses 'Golo', 'Nane' and 'Babeto', while the father uses 'Calendulo', 'Pacho' and 'Gurubaro'.

It is often said by Mexicans that their nicknaming system is more original and more elaborated than that used in peninsular Spain, though in each sub-culture nicknaming flourishes. The more pedestrian character of Spanish naming emerges too in petnaming which seems to be very largely internally motivated and derived simply by obvious syllabic deletions. For example, one Spanish family offer the following list for their seven children: 'Antonia' to 'Tobi', 'Pilar' to 'Piluca', 'Ignacio' to 'Nay', 'Raimond' to 'Monete', 'Santiago' to 'Tito', 'Alberto' to 'Teto' and 'José Maria' to 'José Mari'. A glance back at the example of Mexican petnaming above illustrates this difference very vividly. However, it would require a much more widespread sampling of the family practices of both countries before we would be bold enough to claim more than anecdotal significance for the differences we have been told about and have ourselves observed.

Etymology*

Clues to the psychological and social effects of petnames can be looked for first in a study of the way the names came to be formed. The way these names are experienced by a child must be studied through name autobiographies, accounts of life with the name in question. In this chapter we are concerned only with etymology.

There seem to be four main ways in which petnames are formed. Using the fundamental distinction between internal formations, those which occur through features of the language; and external formations, those deriving from matters outside language, we find that there are two internal modes and two external.

Internal

Parentally created contractions: this part of our study is confined to the English-speaking world, in which it seems clear that a mark of affection, intimacy and closeness of social bond is to use some form of contraction. Thus we have 'Phillip' going into 'Pip', 'Joseph' into 'Joe' into 'Jo-jo'. The latter formation, repetition of a single syllable to mark affection or intimacy is common practice among English speakers. More specifically British, we are inclined to feel, is the formation 'Rachael' to 'Raggers', drawing on a remnant of Oxbridge slang formations of the 1930s, some of which still survives. For example, the Oxford Rugby Cup Competition is still being called 'Cuppers'.

* We owe a great deal in this section to an excellent empirical study by Jonathan Bye.

Child-created formations: children have difficulty pronouncing their names even when they know them well. Their efforts can catch the parental ear, and then be further reformulated. For instance we have record of 'John' going to 'Om' by babytalk, and then being further developed by a common internal process to 'Omlette'. We would like to record that the bearer of the unusual name of 'Sunshine' made 'Dada' from it, and this was taken up and became the petname. The babytalk versions offered by siblings can also act as sources of petnames. There are many commonplace examples, but we noticed the unfortunate 'Phillip' to 'Wee-wee' prompted by the babytalk version of a slightly older brother.

A much rarer formation derives from the child's mispronunciation of a favourite word. We have, for example, the petname 'Ellie' derived from 'Eletant', the babytalk version of 'Elephant'; and another 'Ellie' derived from 'Ellow', which is babytalk for 'Yellow'. And an 'Emmie', not derived from 'Emma', but from 'Ember', which is babytalk for 'Remember'.

External

Interestingly external modes of formation used in the family for pet-names are identical with the well-known modes in the playground formation of nicknames.

From physical attributes: we record the unflattering 'Toad', derived from the appreciative remark of a visiting relative, 'Oh what a lovely little toad!' and the petname 'Pud', indicative of many others like it, called forth by the unusual plumpness of babies. The most remarkable we have on record is the name 'Oddball', used by the members of the family for an unfortunate boy born with only one testicle.

Just as nicknames can become the permanent record of occasions, so too can petnames. The name 'Jig' derived from an occasion when, as a result of violent jigging of the pram an infant managed to throw her-self right out. Family consternation was evidently enough to 'fix' the name.

The relative distribution of these methods strongly favours the child's efforts to pronounce its own name as a source for petnames. The other modes of formation, set out above, offer nothing particularly novel with respect to the methods we will encounter used in the form-ation of nicknames among children, though the children use a wider variety of methods and often make more flamboyant and original use of those instanced above.

Some of these names reverberate down the rest of a person's life course, but we are unable to say from our present studies under what circumstances this occurs, and whether certain kinds of names or certain kinds of people are more prone to this life consequence than others. So far as we are able to discern, the preservation of a petname is pretty much a matter of accident, involving such chance events as a name-conscious friend overhearing a family parley, or a close sibling bringing a particularly striking petname to school.

There seems to be considerable variation in the multiplicity and richness of petnaming practices from family to family. Some families have one or two which quickly become fixed, while others have a flourishing and continuously renewed nomenclature. As an example of a family with an extreme richness of petnames, we can instance the case of a family in New South Wales. We have the following accounts from family members in which the father is clearly identified as the name-giver. Even before they were married the husband-to-be had given his fiancée the name 'Pookie', which she disliked but tolerated. But he had also given her the name 'Poombie' which she very much disliked and actively discouraged because she thought it made her sound fat. Their daughter, Christine, even at the age of nine, was given the name 'Columbus' by the father. The formation was made via the equivalent boy's name 'Christopher' and then by popular association to 'Columbus'. At about the same time Christine was also given the name 'Spaghetti legs' by her father, which, not unnaturally, she disliked rather a lot. One of her brothers, Greg, was given the petname 'Benedictus'. The explanation seems to be that though the family surname had been Greek it had been changed by deedpoll to the homophonous 'Bennett'. By sharing a syllable and tacking on a Mediterranean-sounding ending, something of a 'Greek' flavour was preserved, which the father was reluctant to lose altogether, despite the children's strong 'Aussie' identification. A younger daughter received the name 'Tilly tales' because of her ability to be provocative. But the father elaborated on this by transformation according to local associations to 'Tilly Divine', the name of a lady of easy virtue notorious in Sydney folklore. The child, of course, much resented this transformation. The younger son, Stephen, was given what was thought to be the Welsh name 'Stef' because they lived in New South Wales.

An obvious pattern emerges from this of the father's domination of that family through petnaming. He was clearly inventing and transforming names to the point at which they could be used to irritate and tease. As we shall show in our study of school playground practices, names play a prominent part in teasing routines. We leave to developmental psychologists the question as to why teasing seems to play such an important part in childhood, be it in school or in family life. It is so elaborated and so ubiquitous, it must play some central role in the growth of a person.

4
The Origins of Nicknames

General Etymology

As we shall show in detail, nicknaming is one of the most important features of children's autonomous social worlds and is perhaps the more striking for its independence of influences stemming in any direct way from adults. Nicknames are invented by children for children and show an elaborate and subtle systematicity. A fundamental distinction in all naming systems is between internal methods of formation whereby a name is generated by some feature of language, such as alliteration or rhyming, and external methods of formation where matters of history, appearance, family relationships, local culture and so on are involved in the genesis of the name.

Internal Formations

Rhymes, contractions, verbal analogues and suffix addition seem to be the commonest ways of forming a nickname by internal methods: 'Colley' yields 'Dolly', 'Patricia' goes to 'Trish' and 'Ramow' to 'Cow'. The Opies have pointed out the extraordinary richness of the nickname-forming affixes, so we get from 'Smith' all of the following: 'Smithy', 'Smithbug', 'Smithoh', 'Smithikins', and even the florid 'Smithykinsbug'. In addition to the Opies' list we note the use of '-rat' as a suffix as in 'Hannarat'. A charming example of internal formation is the case of the English Test cricketer, Chris Old, that is 'C. Old', who is clearly 'Chilly'.

External Formations

There seem to be five basic principles at work in the genesis of nicknames by external methods.

1 The recognition of qualities: physical, intellectual and character-
logical attributes can be the basis of the created name. An excellent
account which one must suppose to be based upon some life experience
of this process in the course of action, can be found in a recent novel
(Le Carré, 1976).

> In the course of that same summer term, the boys paid Jim the
> compliment of a nickname. They had several shots before they
> were happy. They tried Trooper, which caught the bit of military
> in him, his occasional, quite harmless cursing and his solitary rambles
> in the Quantocks. All the same Trooper didn't stick, so they tried
> Pirate and for a while Goulash. Goulash because of his taste for hot
> food, the smell of curries and onions and paprike that greeted them
> in warm puffs as they filed past the Dip on their way to Evensong.
> Goulash for his perfect French which was held to have a slushy
> quality. Spikely of Five B could imitate it to a hair: 'You heard the
> question, Berger. What is Emile looking at?'—a convulsive jerk of the
> right hand—'Don't gawp at me, old boy, I'm not a juju man. *Qu'est-
> ce qu'il regarde, Emile, dans le tableau tu as sous le nez? Mon cher
> Berger*, if you do not very soon summon one lucid sentence of
> French, *je te mettrai toute de suite à la porte, tu comprends*, you
> beastly toad?'
>
> But these terrible threats were never carried out, neither in
> French nor English. In a quaint way, they actually added to the aura
> of gentleness which quickly surrounded him, a gentleness only
> possible in big men seen through the eyes of boys.
>
> Yet Goulash didn't satisfy them either. It lacked the hint of
> strength contained. It took no account of Jim's passionate English-
> ness, which was the only subject where he could be relied on to
> waste time. Toad Spikely had only to venture one disparaging
> comment on the monarchy, extol the joys of some foreign country,
> preferably a hot one, for Jim to colour sharply and snap out a good
> three minutes' worth on the privilege of being born an Englishman.
> He knew they were teasing him but he was unable not to rise. . . .
>
> Finally, they hit on Rhino.
>
> Partly that was a play on Prideaux, partly a reference to his taste
> for living off the land and his appetite for physical exercise which
> they noted constantly. Shivering in the shower queue first thing in
> the morning they would see the Rhino pounding down Combe Lane
> with a rucksack on his crooked back as he returned from his morning
> march. Going to bed they could glimpse his lonely shadow through
> the perspex roof of the fives court as the Rhino tirelessly attacked
> the concrete wall. . . .

A real example would be the name 'Kiki' for a teacher who looked like a frog. The physical appearance of the teacher must lead beyond 'Froggy' if there is available a well-known television frog called 'Kiki'.

2   Lévi-Strauss has remarked how famous or striking incidents may be marked in various ways. Amongst children the marking may be achieved by the derivation of a name. For example, during a French lesson one child in reading from the set book, found herself every time it was her turn, with the phrase, '*Jamais*'. Her previously anonymous status was remedied and from then on she became 'Jam'. A boy, at the awkward, adolescent stage for voice control, reading his French set book, was embarrassed by his voice breaking on the word, '*coupable*' and from then on bore the otherwise mysterious name 'Coop'.

3   Another main category of naming methods is the partially externally motivated, where the naming sequence begins with a transition that depends upon a verbal analogy. Such an alliterative sequence begins with the step from 'Jackie Amos' to 'A mosquito' and then by an externally motivated step to 'Flea' since both mosquitoes and fleas are insects in childish entymology.

4   Another large category of formations are based on what one might describe as cultural stereotypes, as for example, where someone called 'Donald' becomes 'Duck' or 'Gordon' changes to 'Flash'.

5   Finally, there are the traditional names, both those associated with particular surnames such as 'Nobby' for 'Clark', 'Dusty' for 'Miller', and those based upon some discernible physical feature such as 'Porky', 'Carrots', 'Stinker', 'Streak' and 'Titch'. The latter are of the greatest importance in the society of childhood and we shall elaborate on their origins and significance in the chapters to come.

Naming in the Junior School

Internally Motivated Formations

Intensive studies of nicknames among children of junior school age, say from six or seven to ten or eleven, show that the largest single class of nicknames are formed by some kind of word-play on given names. About half the total number of nicknames among the thousands we have studied were formed, in part at least, in this way.

Phonetic derivatives
1   Immediate rhyme: 'Harris' to 'Paris'
2   Phonetic similarity:
    (i) To a suitably obnoxious word: 'Britchford' to 'Britches', 'Suresh', to 'Sewers', 'Rayleigh-Marshall' to 'Razamataz'.
    (ii) To another name: 'Loretta' to 'Larry', 'McGowan' to 'McGoo'.
    (iii) From initials: 'R.P.' to 'Harpy', 'P.T.' to 'Phys' and, even by

anagram on initials, from 'A.J.W.S.' to 'Jaws'.

3 Persisting babytalk petname: 'Cuthbert' to 'Cuffy', 'Sharon' to 'Shagger'.

Semantic derivatives

1 Semantic inversion: 'Winterflood' to 'Summerdrought', 'King' to 'Queen(y)'.

2 There are some formations which develop through two or more steps, the first internally motivated, and the second externally. For instance, 'Keith' to 'Beef' to 'Broth'; 'Underwood' to 'Underwear' to 'Y-front'.

Traditional suffix

The Opies list '-ass', '-bug', '-cat', '-dick', '-gog', '-ies', '-sy', '-ey'. In addition, we report the use of '-oh' and '-rat'. These may appear not only as transforming the given name, but as secondary in internally motivated transformations on a nickname, as in 'Bog', to 'Boggoh' and to 'Bograt'.

Semantic affix

'Day' to 'Monday', 'Martin' to 'Housemartin' to 'Housey'.

We have found that the smaller the school class the more internal motivations played some part in the formation of the nicknames. If this is a widespread effect we are quite unable to account for it. Comparing two classes of the same age, in the smaller nearly 60 per cent of the nicknames involved internal motivations in one way or another, while in a class double the size in a nearby part of the country and of roughly the same social mix the proportion had dropped to 40 per cent.

Externally Motivated Formations

Deviation from 'normal' physical appearance

1 Weight:
    (i) pejorative: 'Fatty', 'Hippo' etc.; 'Oxfam', 'Crow', 'Tapeworm-woman'.
    (ii) affectionate: 'Rose-tub', 'Cuddly', etc.; 'Twiggy'.

Jonathan Bye found, in his study, that at the top end of the junior school age-group, that is at around eleven to twelve, greater odium attached to being too thin than to being too fat. Unfortunately, we have been unable to pursue this line of study further, though various explanations suggest themselves. There should be an inversion at the next age-stage, if the idea that there are social factors at work in *anorexia nervosa* is correct.

    (iii) As in other categories, there is secondary elaboration: 'Barrell' to 'Red Barrell' to 'Red', 'Broad' to 'Broad Bean' to 'Bean'.

2 Hair-colour: 'Snow', 'Rusty', 'Carrots', 'Copper-knob' and that Australian curiosity 'Bluey'.

3 Height: 'Big John' for someone small, 'Legs' for someone tall.

4 Uncleanliness: 'Sewage', 'Stinker', 'Pooh' etc.

5 Intelligence: 'Prof', 'Brain-box' and the recent 'Computer' and 'Calculator'.

6 General Appearance: 'Ape', 'Basil', 'Freda' (from 'Frank' to mark femininity).

7 Other aspects of physical appearance: 'Mouthey' for someone with a big mouth. We are happy to report the appearance of 'Concorde' for someone with a large nose.

Personal habits, tastes and character

There are many obvious derivatives, such as 'Fudge' for someone who was conspicuously fond of that sweetmeat. Those who talked more than the usual run of the class tended to have pejorative nicknames such as 'Rattlesnake'. A child who used to bite in playground scuffles became 'Tiger', one who always did messy work became 'Smudge'.

Biographical events

There are rather fewer of these names in our samples than we had expected from our own experiences. We notice such names as 'Nettles' for someone once caught smoking them, and 'Spas' from 'Spastic' for someone who had once broken an arm.

Culturally specific associations

1 Semantic connection: 'Sherrif' to 'Shot-gun' to 'Shotty', 'Parker' to 'Coat', 'Brayfield' to 'Hayfield' to 'Haybag', 'Smart' to 'Chic'.

2 Products: 'Goulden' to 'Golden' to 'Wonder-crisps' to 'Wonder', 'Ambrose' to 'Creamed Rice' to 'Creamy', 'Myers' to 'Myers Divan' to 'Bed' to 'Bed-bug'.

3 TV and film characters: 'Gonzales' to 'Speedy', 'Frankie' to 'Frankie Abbott' to 'Abbott', 'Sharples' to 'Ena Sharples' to 'Ena'.

Nicknaming in a specific tradition

As might have been expected, we still found 'Dusty Miller', 'Nobby Clarke' and 'Tug Wilson'.

Family tradition

Often the origins of these nicknames are lost: 'Dill', 'Wig', etc.

Naming in the Senior School

In a now classical study Peevers and Secord (1974) presented evidence for the idea that as children grow older they take more account of the characters of their friends and acquaintances and less of their possessions. Similarly physical appearance seems to be of little interest to young children, of great importance to adolescents and only begins to fall from its position of central salience among young adults, where personal style becomes of greater importance. Though we shall see some reflections of the Peevers and Secord thesis in the use to which nicknames are put at different ages, apart from a general growth in sophistication and knowledge of the world, the formation processes in use among adolescents are not essentially different from those in favour with the denizens of junior school. Following our general use of the intensive design we present the layout of the formations of one senior school, though we shall be drawing on a wider base of information in our social analysis. But we are satisfied that the pattern we report here is repeated with only minor variations in all the schools and communities we have studied.

Internal Motivation

1 Rhyme: 'Hackett' to 'Bracket'.
2 Semantic association: 'Gardner' to 'Weed'.
3 Traditional suffix: 'Thompson' to 'Thomscrap', 'Timothy' to Timboh'.
4 Cross-linguistic pun: 'Rozee' to 'Dewdrop'.
5 Semantic inversion: 'Sharples' to 'Bluntles'.
6 Historical association: 'Newton' to 'Isaac', 'Burley' to 'Walter'.

External Motivation

1 Personal appearance: 'Spot' (acne), 'Dumbo' (large ears), 'Spantoy' spoken with an Oriental accent (slant eyes), 'Bandy' (legs), 'Joe 90' (glasses), 'Squeaker' (voice), 'Ginger' (hair), 'Snorter' and 'Piggy' (brothers with retroussé noses), 'Berry' to 'Benny' (speech defect), 'Claw' from 'Bird' from 'Beak' (long nose), 'Digby', old English sheepdog (long hair), 'Tench' (big lips), 'Rabbit' (protruding teeth), 'Quasimodo' (humpback).
2 Traditional slots: 'Barrel', 'Frank' (from 'Cannon'), 'Slobadob', 'Apeman', 'Prof', 'Pustulence'.
3 Personal style: 'Bovva' (aggressive), 'Tavna', tough pronunciation of 'Taverner', 'Fiver' from the rabbit in *Watership Down*.
4 Cultural association: 'Jam Butty' for a northerner, 'Alf' (Garnett) for a West Ham supporter.

Though the methods of formation are essentially the same as in the junior school the distribution is markedly different. In the junior school the predominant mode is internal, deriving the nickname from the given name by some purely linguistic transformation, motivated one might say by a delight in playing with language, in the only area where free creation is allowed. But in the senior school physical appearance and personal habits become the dominant source of names. We shall be exploring the meaning of this in the next chapter where we turn to the social force and psychological function of this elaborate social practice.

Multiple Nicknames

In our analysis so far we have proceeded as if each person had one and only one nickname. But we have found that while one name may bear the most social potency and fatefulness for an individual, in those societies where nicknaming is strongly established and flourishing, names proliferate in a florid fountaining of linguistic creativity.

The principles of name creation are conserved, however, since so far as we have been able to find, the same methods of creating names are used to multiply a person's appellations as are used to invent the names for a multiplicity of different people. For instance, a large, dark girl called 'Alison' is reported as having been given the following set of names, almost simultaneously, in a society where nicknaming was well established.

1   Physical characteristics, ironical
'Kitten', 'Chick', 'Muffin' (though this latter may have some connection, since lost, with Muffin the Mule)

2   Biographical incidents
'Jam', a name whose etymology is discussed in an earlier section (p. oo), and 'TPPQ', The Petrol Pump Queen, whose etymology has not been disclosed to us.

3   Name modulation
    'Alison'- 'Ali' - 'Algy' - 'Bilge Pond'
        'Ali' - 'Aligator' - 'Crocodile'
        'Ali' - 'Aluminium'.

4   By a combination of 1 and 3 we get 'Ali' — 'Mahomed Ali' and there is some possibility that the name 'Cassius Clay' which we have classified under 1 should perhaps be regarded as a derivative from 'Mahomed Ali'.

As we shall be demonstrating, multiple nicknames have an important social function in maintaining the fine structure of the social classes within a society, enabling the most powerful groups to maintain their integrity by the use of some sub-class of the total available nicknames.

Name-Trajectories

The Persistence of a Nickname from One School to Another

In other parts of this work we have looked at how nicknames have their uses in a whole range of different social worlds. Different names may be used by the different social groups to which the child belongs. There is another aspect of this phenomenon to be examined: do nicknames persist through the course of a child's development as well as flourishing at particular stages? And if there is some continuity in the naming, how is this achieved?

Here we look rather more specifically at the persistence of nicknames from one school to another—from the lower age-group to the higher. The material here is largely drawn from transmissions observed when children pass from prep and junior schools to their independent secondary schools.

The first observation to be made is purely statistical. From our sample we find that 40 per cent of the pupils report that at least one of their nicknames has been carried from one school to another. This is a high figure considering the fact that, unlike the state sector, those going into independent schools do not necessarily choose a school that is geographically the closest to home. Indeed, those pupils living within ten miles of home are in the minority.

Our next task is to attempt some breakdown of this total by simply asking the question, 'How did your nickname come to your present school if it is the same as a nickname that you had in your last school?'

For the sake of convenience and clarity we will lay out the results in five sections, since they seem to fall into five broad categories:

1 Fifty-seven per cent of all those who report that they do have a nickname in their present school that is the same as a nickname that they had in a previous school maintain that the apparent transmission is by chance. The names in this category are names which, almost without exception, are straightforward formations from the real names of the person concerned, and human creativity at the popular level being what it is, it is not surprising that the names – the same names – have been chosen independently a second time.

Some of the pupils write as follows:

From someone surnamed Leigh:

'Flea. It just happened to be chosen for a second time.'

From someone surnamed Staniland:

'Stan. It just goes with my name—a sort of coincidence.'

From someone with a surname Gladstone:

'Gladys. Since my name is Gladstone, I suppose my nickname came from the "Glad" part of my name, with the "ys" added on.'

From someone with the surname Mills:

'Yes—I have lots of nicknames carried on—anything that rhymes with Mills (Pills, Hills, etc.). People have no imagination in thinking up different sounding names.'

2 Thirty-one per cent of the sample report that the carry-over of their nicknames has been effected by being 'leaked' by a present pupil at the secondary school who was also at the same prep school:

'My nickname "Taurus" has been carried through from my prep school by a friend from the same school, and now it is used by three or four people.'

'Someone in the prep school was here.'

'It was nearly carried on when a friend from my last school told his sister, Jo, who is at this school.'

The most unfortunate case of which we have record is of a girl, happy to transfer with her brother to a new school, who was introduced there by that brother, as 'Gusty', with the gloss, 'She's called that because she's so disgusting', and further elaborated by the inexorable relating of the anecdote that as a baby she was made to eat naked because she threw her food about.

These last three categories represent only small variations though they may be highly significant for individuals. Together they account for less than 12 per cent of the sample:

3 Inheriting a 'family' name. Other members of the same family who came to the school have left names behind them which are inherited by their juniors: 'My cousin had the nickname "Civ" [the surname is Civil] and now I have it.' 'The name "Looney" was first applied to my eldest brother when he was at this school. It's become a sort of family thing. My younger brother gets it sometimes as well.'

The longest-running family nickname we know of is reported from New Zealand where the thirteenth 'Jiggs' Poole is now at Kings College, Auckland, a private boarding school modelled on the lines of an English 'public' school. The first 'Jiggs' was named in 1939 by a fellow member of his boarding house, because of the way his reddish back hair grew out like the hair of the character 'Jiggs' in the well-known cartoon 'Bringing up Father'. This choice of name seems to have been partly internally motivated since we believe that the full initials of the original bearer of the name were 'J.G.S.'.

4 Some people try to get one of their nicknames from a previous school carried over into their present school by their own efforts. Only in rare cases does this seem to work:

'I asked to be called "Monty" (my nickname at my last school) when I came here at first, but they only called me "Mog", and then "Duck" and "Doze".'

5 Finally we come to those names (very few) which have the greatest element of chance—and even then, there may be less chance than there appears. One pupil reports that he has been called 'Prick' at

both his schools, and puts this down to 'coincidence'!

Table 1

Cause of name carrying over	%
Straightforward nickname from real name just happening to be the same name as previously	57
Nickname is 'let out' by a friend who knew	31
Inheriting a family name	4
Attempted self-selection of nickname	4
Coincidence	4

5
The Creation and Maintenance of Social Classes

Introduction

We shall show how the nicknaming system is powerfully influential in generating and maintaining the social order that children create for themselves in their own autonomous society. Broadly speaking, it seems to have two main functions and several secondary uses:

First, the creation and maintenance of social classes within the externally created groupings imposed upon children by adults; and second, the promulgation and sustaining of norms of appearance and behaviour. In this chapter we turn our attention to the role of nicknaming in the autonomous creation by children of a fine structure of social classes within the institutional groupings imposed upon them.

In general the nicknaming system seems to effect three main divisions:
1 People and non-people. It marks those who are rejected altogether from the social order prevailing in a particular children's group, the untouchables or non-persons. They have no nicknames, or where nicknaming is not the rule they are the only ones with nicknames.
2 It is used to mark off the well-knit groups who have some kind of privileged position in the society by the simple device of a set of names used and usable (and sometimes only known) by the members of that group. For example, amongst thirteen-year-old girls a tightly knit group with certain musical privileges used the names 'Jam', 'Chocky', 'Felix', 'Porky' and 'Phlea'. (This curious spelling of 'Flea' is explained by Phlea as follows: 'I don't want to be associated with those nasty little bugs!) Only group members could safely use these names though they were known by others. Expulsion, even temporally, from the group, was marked by a return to given name.
3 Finally, there is the process by which scapegoats are created, a process centred round the spreading of the use of pejorative nicknames, sometimes from the traditional stock. This process we have called

'slotting'. As a recipient of a traditional pejorative nickname an individual may be forced into a social group which, unlike that of the non-person's, forms a part of the society and is in constant, if painful, interaction with the other members, and even with high status members of the 'people'. The scapegoats are abused, teased and generally ritually humiliated, but are often kept quite close to the most powerful group in the society.

Each of these processes of class formation and marking deserves closer examination.

Names and No-Names

The nicknaming system allows for a double division of children. The broadest division is into those with nicknames and those without, the non-people. Non-people are so 'weedy' they are beyond contempt. Then those with nicknames are more finely sub-divided into the acceptable and the stigmatised, the scapegoats. But our observations and conversations with the natives suggest that it is better to be stigmatized than to be a non-person, for not to exist socially is the worst fate of all. We illustrate this with a beautiful 'fictional' example, from *David and Broccoli*, by John Mortimer (1973).

> David Golanski is a typical 'weed' and therefore very unhappy in his equally typical male, rugger-playing, cold-shower-taking, public school. Having just proved his cowardice beyond question in a recent boxing lesson, he is summoned to the Head's study:
>
> *Headmaster*: Come in, Golansky. My wife's just doing a little job. . . Quite the man about the house. . . (He laughs). You don't mind if 'Chippy' stays for our chat?. . .
>
> *David*: No.
>
> *Headmaster*: You see. We know the nicknames you boys give us. My wife is 'Chippy'. You call me 'Hercules' . . . no doubt because of my labours!?
>
> *David*: No. I. . . .
>
> *Headmaster*: Don't worry, Golansky. Good heavens! It's only part of the atmosphere and shows the school is a well-run and happy ship! 'Chippy', 'Hercules'. . . and our well-loved professional is 'Broccoli', isn't he? What do they call you?
>
> *David*: Golansky, Sir.
>
> *Headmaster* (Shocked): Your real name?
>
> *David* (Miserably): Yes.
>
> *Headmaster*: You see! I'm afraid you haven't quite fitted in among us yet. Not quite had your corners rubbed off, shall we say?

But the significance of having no nickname depends upon the strength and ubiquity of the nicknaming system as a social practice. There seem to be considerable differences between schools in different parts of the world and this we think can be readily related to the social nature of the school, that is to its relations to the community which it serves. As we shall show, the grey area of 'non-persons' is not necessarily typical of every institution. Of importance to us in this chapter is the fact that in the boarding school we chose as fulfilling the requirements of an ideal subject of study according to the intensive design, there seemed to be no one who managed to avoid a nickname, or perhaps we should say everyone had succeeded in acquiring one. But in some schools, particularly in the United States, there are no nicknames in use at all. Why is there this difference in the nicknaming practices in different schools and what does it tell us about them as institutions?

We can begin by reminding ourselves that the facts seem to be these: in the public (i.e. private) boarding school, no one was without a nickname, while in a state day school in England there seemed to be a proportion of each form or school class, generally about 20 per cent, who were quite without nicknames of any kind. We found that in America, at least in the north-east, mid-west and west, nicknames were rare or even unknown in the state school system, at all ages. Extensive enquiries in some twenty states failed to turn up evidence of any elaborated systems at all. While this spread of different social naming practices is vast, we have to consider the possibility that it is a chance phenomenon, an artefact of the sampling method we have employed to find cases for intensive study according to the prescriptions of the ethogenic method.

However, we can rule out chance on two grounds. A glance at the range of naming systems we have studied in preparing this book is enough to show that our sampling has been both wide and deep. On purely statistical grounds, for those who set store by such things, we can have some confidence in our conclusions. More important, however, from a scientific point of view, is the correlation between the naming systems and the social structure of the various institutions in which they are found, that is the one becomes intelligible in terms of the other.

Let us look at this more closely. The public boarding school would approximate more nearly to Goffman's definition of a *total institution*. Goffman, in his study of the social life of mental hospitals and other places of refuge and confinement (1961), suggests that the following features are characteristic of what he considers the typical closed institution:

(i)   The institution is a place of both residence and work.
(ii) It contains a large number of individuals of similar status.
(iii) The inmates stay there for long periods.

(iv)   The life-style is enclosed and formally administered.

(v)   The inmates are cut off from the main-stream of civil life.

Though there are similarities, the boarding school diverges from this pattern in several respects.

(i)   The school receives new entrants each term.

(ii)   The holidays are quite substantial and are spent away from school.

(iii)   There is usually a fairly pronounced hierarchy, even in official terms, amongst the pupils themselves.

These differences are significant, but they do not prevent nick-naming being far richer than it would otherwise be if the institution were totally open and outward-looking. For practical purposes the necessities of the administration of even a partially closed social entity mean that it is very difficult for the school to do otherwise than approximate to Goffman's typical 'asylum'.

The approximation of the average state day school to a Goffmanian total institution is so minimal that there is little opportunity for a rich underlife to develop with its own social classes and with nicknaming as one of the means of maintaining them.

The local order is quite different. For the pupils of the state day school, the school buildings are a place of work only. When the bell rings at 4 o'clock, the inmates return to their homes. It is at home that they do most of their eating, sleeping, homework and television-watching. This also means that the pupil of the day school rarely spends the protracted periods away from home that is characteristic of boarding education. On the practical side, the organisation in the boarding school will be a thing which necessarily extends over all the possible aspects of daily life, including eating and sleeping, which in the day school are largely catered for in the home. The life of the average day-school pupil will therefore tend to be less formally administered than the pupil of the boarding school. The day school approximates very imperfectly to Goffman's model of a 'total institution'.

When we come to consider the American equivalent to our English state day school (often for the British, confusingly called a 'public school'), the situation is different again. It would clearly be precarious to attempt to sketch in a short space the details of both the American way of life and their system of education, so we shall content ourselves with a thumb-nail sketch of the feel of the typical American secondary school. This is best done by contrast.

Even in the English day school there is still (despite the efforts of some local education authorities) a great gulf placed between the school and the rest of the community. Few parents would think of walking into the school where their children are being educated, and just having a casual look around. The feeling is, in general, that parents must leave their offspring at the school gates and stay out unless specially invited in. The headmaster is, of course (at least if he is prudent) also a public relations man. He holds specially prepared open days and parents' evenings. He also will have a parents' committee, which will make suggestions and, it is hoped, raise money by Christmas fairs and the like. Nevertheless, he is under absolutely no obligation whatsoever to even have a parents' committee, let alone to pay any attention to their suggestions. The teacher is the respected professional, and 'teacher knows best'. Mums and Dads must sit and dote.

Things are different in America. Without going into the details of the American educational system we can say that the parents in the American school have a statutory part to play in the administration and finance of 'state' education. The boot is very definitely on the other foot. This greater amount of direct outside control of the school is coupled with a general difference in social attitudes. The American school is much more closely integrated into the community as a whole, which means that, of the three cases that we have been discussing, the American secondary school is as an institution the weakest approximation to the Goffman 'asylum'. The American secondary school can often have only a minimal feeling of social cohesion about it.

We have now sketched, albeit briefly, the social character of the three different institutions. All that remains is to put our two sets of facts together and see if there is any correlation between them.

We have three nicknaming systems:

(i)   which allows no one to escape;

(ii)   which labels only 70 per cent or 80 per cent of those who live within it;

(iii)   and, at the other extreme, where almost no one gets a nickname.

Against this sliding scale of nicknaming differences is what we believe is a corresponding range of types of social cohesion. The public boarding school is a very close, intensively organised institution where individual members are thrown together in close proximity for extended periods. The English day school is not by any means as intense. The pupil can escape home in the evenings and lick whatever wounds he or she may have acquired, in the privacy of the home, and, no doubt, under an indulgent parental eye. The American secondary school could hardly, we think, be called intense at all.

From this we can reasonably conclude that the intensity of the nicknaming system is related to the intensity of the social structure. By this we mean that the comprehensiveness of the nicknaming system seems to vary in proportion to the type of social control which characterises the institution.

This relationship is not quite as straightforward as it might at first sight appear. In our description of the types of institution which we gave above, we concentrated primarily on a description of the external aspects of the institution—the sort of administration, the number of meals eaten there, the length of time spent there. Nicknames, however, are not given by the *official* administration of the given institution, or at least not often.

What happens, we think, is this: the type of social control—that is, *official* social control in the school—acts as the determining set of factors, along with the school's position *vis-à-vis* society at large, and sets the conditions under which the children may interact. The public (i.e. independent) school system forces its inmates into relatively close and prolonged contact with each other, so that the autonomous child-child world is very prominent. In the American school the amount of time any one social group will spend together will be significantly smaller, and consequently this autonomous child-child world will be diminished in importance. As it is this child-child world that is largely responsible for the giving of nicknames, this accounts for the differences we have found. Thus the extent and nature of the child-child world is determined by the nature of the institution which contains it, and this further accounts for the correlation between external social characteristics of the institution and its naming system.

We should like to mention briefly in passing another phenomenon which is closely linked with the named/un-named boundary. The researches we have carried out suggest that the number of nicknames a child receives can be quite staggering. It would be unusual for any named child to have only a single nickname. Some children have twenty or more names in use at any one time. These very high numbers are not the norm, although the average number of names which children receive is considerably higher than the casual outside observer might think.

If we take the total number of nicknames in use in any class in a school, and divide this number by the number of people in the class, we shall arrive at an average figure, which we shall call the 'name density'. From the work that has so far been completed, it seems certain that the trend is for the nicknaming density to be highest where the institution approximates best to Goffman's 'total institution'.

Better a Derogatory Name than No Name at all

Depersonalisation through being nameless is a miserable state. In an earlier study (Harré, 1976) we found that, particularly among West Indian and Pakistani children, having to answer to even a foul or derogatory nickname was perceived as better than having no eke-name at all. In our present work we have been able to draw upon a close case study of this phenomenon.* Using the techniques of sociogram representation

*The study we report here is due to Sarah Davis.

we can express the social relationships between a small group of girls and match these to their nicknames. The case concerns a group of four girls whose nicknames for each other are 'Puss' (used for two of them), 'Gnome', 'Brains or Mac' and 'Smell' or 'Snoteater'. We have drawn out the relationship structure of this group in Figure 2 to show how one person, S.J., although in the group, is not quite as strongly attached as the rest. Her nicknames, 'Smell' and 'Snoteater' are surprising until we learn (a) that her first name is Sonita (and therefore ripe for trans-formation to the last nickname) and (b) that she is dark-skinned. In our earlier studies we found that though West Indian children were often given derogatory nicknames they perceived this as better than having none. Being abused, they were at least noticed. In giving them a dero-gatory nickname the other children were able to fulful their need to use someone as a scapegoat, (and a black child is an obvious target in a pre-dominantly white group), and at the same time find a way of accepting him into the group. It might be a way of resolving a conflict between liking him/her as an individual but being required ritually to condemn his skin colour (perhaps because of feelings from adult society filtering down to our children).

We notice here, for the first time, the marking of a strong bond by calling each other by the same or very nearly the same name, in the case of 'Puss'.

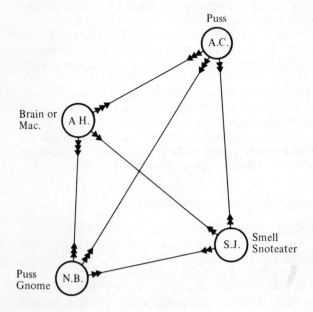

Figure 2

The Fine Structure of the Social Order : Friends

What of the smaller social units in general? Can their boundaries be firmly defined by the labels with which each group attempts to structure itself over against the social environment? Taking one primary class for intensive study, we revealed a strong match between the name-structure and a sociogram of friendship groupings. The latter was given to us as follows: (using official names)

A   Joanne   Ruth   Wendy   Julie
B   Sharon   Mandy   Margaret   Lynn   Debbie   Teresa   Louise

C   Adam   Nigel   Michael
D   Stephen   Steven S.   Stewart
E   Ali   Peter   Roy
F   Paul

Misc.   Ronnie, Derek, Ricky, Garry G., Garry P., Robert, Oliver, Richard, Raymond (randomly and occasionally distributed between A and C).

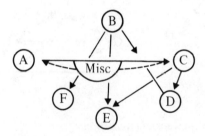

Figure 3   Sociogram of perceived prestige rankings

The children were asked to complete individual nickname registers of their class and these were then compared to see whether set by set they cohered to produce groupings matching the friendship groups identified independently. The results were apparently inconclusive—a strong naming structure in one group immediately being counteracted by diversity and weakness in the next. Further investigation through the teacher who had worked on preparing the sociometric map revealed that the strength or weakness of the naming system was related to the fluidity of friendship-sets. Many such sets, while strongly perceived for a short while, especially at primary level, do not crystallise sufficiently to acquire the acknowledgment implied by representation in a nickname system.

Even when the nicknames themselves are not explicit and systematic representations of the social structure, their presence or absence does distinguish broadly different types of community and can also shade in the colours of a friendship map within the class. A sociometric analysis of a much older class in a mixed comprehensive, for instance, reads like this:

A   Debra Jackie Louise Donna
B   Tina Jane Elaine Brenda
C   Julia Audrey Debra Anna Kim
D   Sharon Lynn
E   Sue Judy
F   Kay Leslie Yvonne Elizabeth

G   Peter Keith Suresh
H   Ian Paul Mark
I   David David Nigel
J   Wayne Gary Raymond Richard

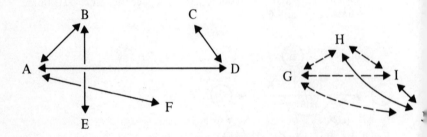

Figure 4 Sociogram of degree of mutual social interaction

Of the seven people without nicknames in this class, five came from one group. This set, while always perfectly friendly with the others, took care throughout the year both to sit and work together. In the twelve months, too, the remainder of the class were noticeably more fluid in their friendships than those in the unnamed category. The relationship of the unnamed was always a more permanent and stable affair. The rest, we argue, tacitly acknowledged this separateness by using their official names rather than inventing nicknames for them.

This correspondence was interesting, but to claim that the greyer areas of general popularity coincided with a deficiency in nicknaming on the basis of research with just one class would have been highly suspect. It deserved, we thought, following up. A wider study of a whole year in a large comprehensive school of a much larger and more diverse population of adolescents revealed that 20 per cent were unnamed by their peers. Form teachers were then asked to categorise class members with no nicknames into three broad groups. The grouping system adopted and the results are given below:

1 Popular   : 20 per cent
2 Minority groups : 60 per cent
3 Isolates   : 20 per cent

As the table indicates, 60 per cent were from this minority group-area —with friends, but incohesive and, to a certain extent, autonomous sub-groupings. Couple this with the overall relationships in this total population of children, which highly correlates popularity with having a good nickname, and isolation with having a bad one, and it is clear that in this case the naming system correlates the 'grey' areas of that society, occupied by those who were neither popular nor unpopular, with a deficiency of nicknames. This suggests that a wide variety of marking systems operate, most drawing *in different ways*, on the socially available machinery, namely nicknaming.

The acknowledgment of a set, however, need not be in a negative mode, marked by the lack of an unofficial name. From a mixed comprehensive we have the following system. We noticed a curious entry for one girl, namely:

Joanne   Dragoon no. 3

Joanne was unable to give an explanation of this, but then we turned up:

Kay   Dragoon no. 7

It emerged that the girls at the local boys' club had been christened by the boys and each had a number. They were much in vogue and had been identified by the boys as a particular set, with idiosyncratic habits, certain social traits, haunts, etc. and their cohesion was recognised by their corporate nicknames. In this case nicknames are used positively to delineate a social set/group from the outside.

Sometimes, too, the naming system can sketch in minute details on the social map. It can give official status to a very close friendship, for instance: Camilla F. cited herself as 'Plum'; Lucy O. as 'Pudding'. The reason for this compound name was supplied by an obliging friend: 'Lucy always goes with Camilla and "plum" always goes with "pudding".' Goffman describes this sort of thing as tie-signs of a 'participation unit', that is a party of more than one whose members are perceived to be together in a social setting—in school context, best friends.

Names can, then, articulate a permanent relationship. They can also highlight the tensions prevalent between two individuals at any one time. A salient example of this was apparent in the class lists submitted by one primary class and to which the following postcript had been added by the teacher: 'As for the worst culprits of nicknaming, I'm not

very sure: most of it occurs at break and dinner time, but I would guess
—Peter W., Ali K., Steven S., and Louise W.' In the light of this information the lists were scrutinised and certain nuances began to emerge.
Some members—Ricky H., Peter W., Lynn R.—had apparently inno-
cently confessed to various versions of 'Ice-cream'. Steven S., Derek R.,
Louise W., Ali K. to names like 'Skin-head', 'Blacky', 'Kojak', 'Enoch'
and 'Nig-nog'. Now as there were obviously more than three Caucasian
children in the form, but these alone cite that particular name, its elite
usage picked out those children apparently indirectly stigmatising the
darker skinned members. But the darker children, interestingly enough,
had turned the stigmas around by a simple inversion of the norm by
their victims. A dark pigment, they asserted, was the norm: pale skin
was an abnormality. In playground games the two factions were highlighted by the names hurled. Further examination of our name lists
shaded in the personalities, relationships and tensions in even finer detail.

Peter W., for instance, was referred to as 'Pete' by the majority.
From Steven S., however, we get 'Fatty' and 'Long-haired Monster' for
Peter W., both implying a good deal of hostility. Steven, it seemed, had
suffered quite recently at Peter's hands, because Louise and Derek,
though also beneficiaries of his stigmatising nicknames, both make far
less cutting comments. Wendy H., by contrast, is unmentioned in the
slanging match, and the teacher links her with a group of 'nice' girls.
To the majority of the class Wendy is 'Hold' or 'Wednesday'—verbal
analogies with her surname. Ali, alone in a list that was practically all
rhyming, claims to call her 'Ice-cream'—perhaps indicating some
personal fracas between these two alone.

Nicknames, by their existence, absence or implication, then, can
shade in the social map of a class, its groups, hostilities and great friendships. They do more, however, than just define social boundaries within
the group. They also correlate roughly with popularity within the
whole group. Ali K., for example, in the class just mentioned, deliberately presented himself as Asian in a 'Black/Ice-Cream'-hurling
environment, but emerged from the various lists without racial stigma,
'Ali Baba' and 'Shorty' being the most vicious to come his way. Interestingly enough, referring back to the sociometric grouping by the
teacher, we find that Ali is, ironically enough, a mate of Peter W.—one
of the main aggressors in the racial nickname conflict. Ali can possibly
enjoy the peace of political friendship, as it were, between the presidents of rival republics, who, as presidents, have more in common than
their rival groups of subjects.

Far more clearly defined is the area of unpopularity and isolation.
From the same intensive study of these nine-year-olds, another feature
of the perceived grouping emerges. Notice that of these groups delineated in Figure 2, only one contains one member. The nicknames
'Four-eyes', 'Goggle-eyes', 'Snotty-nose' are all levelled at Paul T. The

various titles are similar in the latent hostility implied, and might give some indication of the reasons for this isolation. Despite his extra pair of eyes Paul did not possess the traditionally acceptable median measure of brain power. As one of the remedials of the class, he tended to need extra tuition, which isolated him even more. The most damaging comment must be that of Adam B. : 'I call him "Short Trousers". He *still* wears short trousers' (very shameful behaviour at the age of nine).

In another primary school, Denise W. was called 'Misery' and 'Flea-bag' by her peers. Her unpopularity is a cause for concern. She tells us that her Mum has told her to ignore the jibes if possible. This she does:

Adult: That's the best, isn't it?
Denise: Yes, but Sharon W., she started pulling my hair yesterday and her Mum came out.
Adult: She shouted at her?
Denise: Yes, she shouted at her, her mother did.
Adult: Well, that's what Mums are for, really, isn't it?

The presence, the absence, the implications of nicknames do seem to correlate in several different areas with social forces, whether group boundaries, class trends, special friendships, recent quarrels, specific prejudices, even an assessment of popularity ratings. The correspondence should not, of course, be over-estimated, though surely it is too consistent a factor to be ruled out as merely coincidence. The tip of the iceberg provided by a name hints at least at the mammoth proportions and the perplexity of the perceptual attitudes, out of sight, beneath the social sea's surface.

For the final study in this section we turned to a very detailed examination of a secondary-school class to see how far the fine structure of friendship groups and their marking by nicknaming persisted into adolescence. The girls who participated in this study were about fourteen years old.*

Nicknames and Social Relationships

Sociograms were built up from the answers to a questionnaire. These questions were answered by each girl for her relationships with every other girl in the class. The social structure that emerged from the analysis of these data is represented in Figure 5.

For the sake of clarity we have let three arrows represent six or more relations, showing a strong link with the person; two arrows represent four or five relations, which shows a fairly good link; one arrow represents two or three relations only, showing little interaction.

*This study was carried out by Sarah Davis.

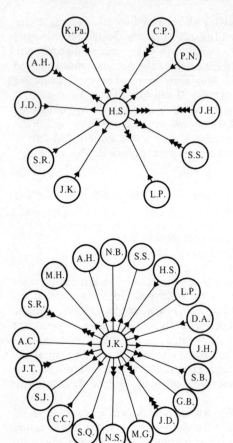

Figure 5

When two, three, or more girls reciprocate arrows equally, we find a group of friends emerging. At the other end of the scale, a lack of arrows and relating lines shows up those who are in isolation from these groups and even from the class as a whole. By consulting the sociogram one can also pick out those who have the most connections spread throughout the class—a finger in every pie, as it were. Such people are likely to emerge as leaders of some sort, or at least as being popular. Finally, one can see who is in the certain, or 'safe', position of having reciprocal intercourse with all or most of the persons to whom she relates, while others send out relating lines, almost hopefully, without receiving any in return, or receive relating lines (unconsciously or not) but do not return any, through lack of desire or in oversight.

By using the following questionnaire,* a comparison between nicknames and a rough test of social attitude to another person was made.

(1) Write down the names of the classmates you would like to sit next to.
(2) Write down those you would never sit next to.
(3) Write down the people you think are clever in your class.
(4) Write down the ones you think are amusing.
(5) Who do you think is naughty but clever?
(6) Who do you consider naughty and a nuisance?

Perceived social relations were examined in discussions based upon the following questions.

(1) Do you bring sweets/food to school?
(2) Who do you share them/it with?
(3) Have you ever been invited to stay by any of your classmates?
(4) Whom have you stayed with?
(5) Are there any people whom you would never stay with, even though invited to?
(6) If so, who?
(7) Whom have you invited to say?
(8) Did they come? If not, who didn't?
(9) Who do you spend most time with in school?
(10) Out of school?
(11) To whom do you lend things?
(12) Whom do you borrow things from?
(13) Do you know the parents of any of your classmates?
(14) If so, which?
(15) Do your own parents know their parents socially?

Several interesting discrepancies emerged. For example, two girls put down derogatory nicknames beside a person they apparently disliked or disapproved of, that person being either unaware of the nickname or refusing to acknowledge its use with reference to herself. This also happened with nicknames that were unflattering but meant with affection. Even a neutral one such as 'Daffy' (from Dyson) appeared to be unknown to the owner but was written by a friend.

There were also examples of girls writing down nicknames of which there was no sign that they were actually used. For example, one girl

*The answers served, of course, as the basis of further accounts elicited by the investigator with the girls as full participants.

wrote for herself, 'Everyone calls me "Hermeseta" but my best friend calls me "Maggot".' Presumably, although 'everyone' might include people outside the class, it must also include those inside the class, and yet nobody attached 'Hermeseta' to her name. But her best friend, as revealed by the sociogram, did indeed write 'Maggot' and nobody else did.

Concerning two nicknames, 'Ethel' of 'Efel' and 'Herman' (from which the aforesaid 'Hermeseta' might also have arisen), there appeared to be some kind of competition. They seem to be more of a classic joke —a standard nickname—of that particular class, rather than a personalised nickname. It is interesting that the girl (H.S.) who had the most nicknames (all of which she also wrote down for herself) claimed both of these names and was, what's more, called one or the other of them by various members of the class.

But apart from these discrepancies people were fairly clear about the nicknames they did know and the owners' beliefs about their own nicknames usually confirmed them. Many who had more than one stated roughly who used which and, on checking this with the written answers, they were found to be correct.

In fact, what had at first appeared to be a somewhat confused or arbitrary behaviour in the matter of nicknaming, revealed itself under closer inspection to be a clear, though complicated system. A newcomer, as in our own adult society, would have to get to know it in order to avoid making a *faux pas*, such as a mere acquaintance using a nickname for someone that is reserved for use by her best friend only.

The point that some knew certain nicknames for some girls, whereas others knew different ones for the same girls, is of particular interest not only because it demonstrates more of the naming system in action, but also because it tells us more about the nature of this system.

Before moving onto the final stages of exploring any relationship between the naming system and the sociological structuring of the class, we should like to mention one more discovery made from the written answers. There was only one girl (H.So.) who either did not know or refused to use anybody else's nickname. The one nickname she wrote down for herself was 'Dear Heart', used by M.K. and indeed, only this one person used it. We shall put forward a modest explanation for this very unusual nickname later.

These two separate pieces of research, when put together, yield the following results:

1   The first thing to notice is a fairly strongly related group as shown by the re-drawn detail of a section of the sociogram, Figure 6.

One can see from this that whereas there are strong connections between G.P. and D.W., C.P. and S.S., and S.S. and J.H., there is only a weak connection between D.W. and S.S., and no connection between J.H. and either of the other two. On turning to the nicknames, one discovers that C.P. calls D.W. 'Diz' and D.W. calls C.P. 'Caz'. S.S. is just in the group (being strongly related to C.P. and is called 'Saz' by C.P. but nothing by D.W. J.H. is also allowed to call S.S. 'Saz' and is perhaps therefore on her way to becoming a fuller member of the group, although she herself has not yet got one of these special names.

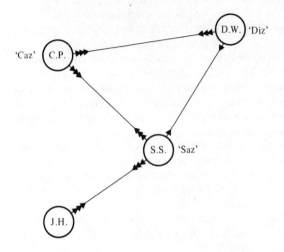

Figure 6

Nobody else uses the names 'Caz' and 'Diz' for these two girls. Indeed, C.P. is generally called 'Pru' (from her surname Purdy).

In this case one can see how 'special' names have been created to mark the special relationship between them. And these 'special' names are all the more striking on account of their alliteration, forcing one to notice the existence of a pattern. They are of the same type we believe we have unearthed in the reciprocal usage of the same name among intimates we noticed above.

2 The sociogram also reveals extreme contrasting social positions. One person, H.S., has been mentioned earlier on in this section. As can be seen from the attached diagrams (Figure 5), J.K. sends out by far the most relating lines—in fact she scores highest in this out of the whole class. J.K. relates herself to eighteen people in the class and H.S., who comes out third in the number of lines each person sends out, relates herself to ten people. It is immediately clear, however, that J.K.'s relating lines are predominantly only 'one-way', i.e. although she sends out eighteen lines, she only receives eight in return. H.S., on the other hand, has no 'one-way' lines. All her relations are reciprocated.

H.S. is outstanding in this because she is the only one in the class who is shown by the sociogram to send out as many lines as she receives.

Her social position is very secure and she probably has a great deal of influence.

This is confirmed by the nicknaming system, for H.S. is the one who has the most nicknames that are also the most widely known and used, two of which are the classic ones, 'Ethel' and 'Herman' (as spoken of earlier), but one of which is 'Selley' or 'Seley' and is used the most.

J.K., on the other hand, although she gives herself a nickname, adding that she is called this 'by two friends (not best)', is not given a nickname by anyone at all on the written answer sheets.

It is not coincidental, we believe, that such an influential member of the class as H.S. should have such a large number of nicknames which are at the same time used very widely and which mark her out linguistically. That there should be a linguistic choice, as it were, allows for all sorts and conditions of people to refer to her, thus making her accessible to the maximum number of people.

Another example of this phenomenon can be seen at a lower scoring level with S.B. and S.Q. S.Q. sends out twelve relating lines, receives only three and has no nicknames either given by herself or used by anyone else. S.B., however, sends out only eight lines but receives eleven. She has three nicknames, 'Bally Hoo', 'Tarzan' and 'Ballantine', with an 'i', which have a jovial flavour about them, slotting her into the role of a clown almost. This may be a reason for the fact that she receives the most relating lines in her class.

3   The last illustration, shown in Figure 7, is concerned with a girl in quite the opposite position to that of H.S. This is the sorry plight of H.So.

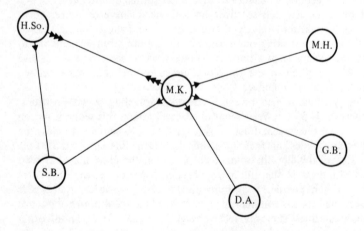

Figure 7

It is perfectly obvious from the sociogram (although we have drawn out her relationship to the class separately for the sake of clarity in Figure 7) that she is the least related person in the class. She sends out only two lines, one strong and one weak, and receives only one in return, although a strong one.

It is most extraordinary how this situation is reflected in the nick-naming system. She is the girl mentioned in the last section as not knowing anybody's nickname in the class or refusing to put them down. Her one nickname for herself, 'Dear Heart', is used by her one strong contact and perhaps such an unusual, intimate and sensitive one for the very reason that she is so isolated otherwise. It is as though her friend is trying hard to compensate for this unenviable position, and in one way possibly succeeds. For, whereas H.So. is content to remain isolated in that she only bothers to send out one other weak relating line besides her strong contact, her friend, M.K., is not content and therefore in a possibly unhappier situation. She is not given a nick-name by her one and only reciprocated relation, although she writes on the self-written slip of paper, 'Nelly or Melon by a few friends'. But at least she does know some of the other class-members' nicknames and is, according to the sociogram, more in contact with the class.

These examples confirm the view that there is a close relation of the social structure of the class to its nicknaming system—related to the extent that, as one has seen illustrated here, nicknames can actively mark out groups or individuals and indeed are often consciously used for this purpose. Children, it should be clear by now, do use linguistic means as one way of sorting out their society.

Our colleague who made this study reports that she was amazed by what she found out from it. It was certainly not apparent from day-to-day classroom contacts that H.So. was so isolated or, in fact, disliked. Miss Davis tells us that if she had known as much about this child's predicament in the beginning as she found out from the study she could perhaps have done something to help.

Furthermore, though she guessed that H.S. was one of the leading characters she had no idea as to the extent of her influence. Miss Davis now believes that one of the reasons she got on so well with this class as a whole was that, quite by chance, she got on well with H.S. She never found her any trouble though some of the other teachers did. It is obviously helpful to be approved of by a leader in the class as this will affect the attitude of the whole class in general.

One can see how it would be possible to deduce a great deal about individual children both from the way they use nicknames and from the actual nicknames themselves, which could be of great help to teachers.

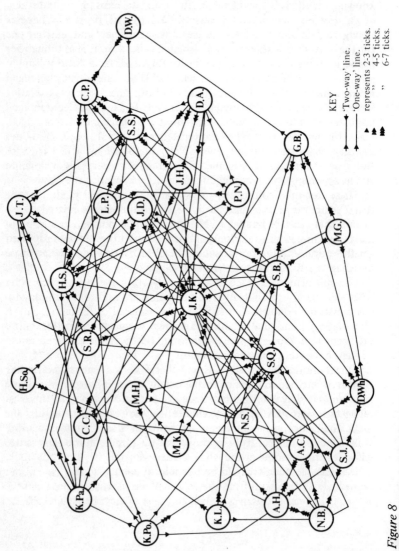

Figure 8

The Fine Structure of the Social Order : Scapegoats

The persistence of traditional nicknames, both those that serve to acknowledge the merit of the attribute they single out and the pejorative and insulting ones, has to be explained. We first supposed that the pejorative nicknames served to create scapegoats. Those who received them were cast as florid examples of various childhood sins such as greed and dirtiness. They could then be safely despised as the bearers of the obloquy which would otherwise be directed upon all or nearly all the members of the tribe. This hypothesis did not explain the persistence of favourable traditional names, but there has turned out to be a measure of truth in it nevertheless. We shall show that traditional nicknames are rather more concerned with the promulgation of social norms than they are with scapegoating, though the latter process does indeed occur. Scapegoats are a discernible social class, closely, even intimately, linked with the most powerful and high status people in the society, but at the same time systematically persecuted and despised.

As we studied various examples of scapegoating and looked more closely at the bearers of the traditional names we became aware of a disparity between the attribute that the nickname would suggest characterised its bearer and the way that child seemed to us as outsiders. It became clear that in the process of acquiring the name the child was forced into a 'slot' for which it was sometimes only marginally prepared through its shape, size or habits. In short, we began to see that 'Fatty' is as much a name of the role of Fatboy as it is a description of the individual who currently fills that role. The process of coming to fill the demands of the nickname could be seen in cases other than the traditional.

We know from ethnographers that there is a tendency for those who originally find themselves in the Eagle totem purely as a representation of the demarcation between them and some other endogamous group, say the Bears, after a time, one might say, becoming and acting like Eagles. A participant ethnographer of tender age, but sharp eyes, reports from an Oxford school of the slow development of a florid display of feline characteristics of behaviour by one who originally acquired the nickname 'Pussy' from the shape of her eyes alone. Thus on analogy with the totem-name case one might expect the attribution of a nickname to prompt a behaviour style that would tend to fill out its implications thus showing the holder to be worthy of the name.

The Chocolate Factory : Nicknames as Weapons in the Race War

Boundaries do not just divide, they have valency, they mark a social direction from 'in' to 'out'. So far we have noticed only those where

contempt is directed outward and fear inward. But in the use of nicknames to mark racial boundaries the two sides use stigmatising names
for each other. Those who may begin as despised and 'out' fight back
and reverse the valency of the boundary by devising rude names for
those who were originally 'within'.

The area of research included an immigrant sector that comprised
about 10 per cent of the total population. Nicknames, we have noted,
highlight the abnormal in a given community. They stigmatise, and in
doing so very often become agents in the process of formulating the
prejudice. To take a pertinent example, racial prejudice is implicit in
varying degrees in all societies today. To articulate this underlying
hostility 'Wops', 'Dagos', 'Froggies', 'Nig-nogs' do more than simply
label. They have 'anti-' connotations. The use of such a name, because
awareness of its implications are universal, cuts deeply. It makes the rift
between the two sides more emphatic and finally unbridgeable.

As in adult society, the various ethnic groups in the classroom were
always carefully labelled and delineated. Like their grown-up counterparts too, the labels did not just categorise, they stigmatised as well.
Despite the similarity in this use of nicknames, the children sensed adult
disapproval and so politely, but firmly, removed it from adult view.
Teachers, particularly at primary level, were often aware of about 50
per cent of the names prevalent in their classes at any one time. Not so
with this. One teacher was able to pinpoint main offenders and reci-
pients but only by observation during her playground duties. The
children's lists gave another side of the picture: in their own inimitable
spelling.

1   Linda P.   – Paradise – Bicues of my name
                 Banoon Face – Bicues of my culer

2   Karen A.   – Cas – Name
               – Alice – Name
               – Halfcast – Bicues of my colour

Because this stigma has now become a social prejudice, it tends to be
deeper hidden from the sight of the adult world. As we have already
noted, Clara received the unequivocal 'Chocolate Drop' when inter-
rupting a skipping game, but would not dream of listing it in a classroom. With this particular area of research, the methods employed,
already subject to the qualifications we have mentioned, must be even
more inadequate here. Only a daily familiarity and nurturing of confidence could reveal a true picture of the situation. This must be
necessarily opaque.

An interesting aspect of the stigma was the way the nicknames reflected folk-prejudices concerning difference between the ethnic groups
in an area. Maxine and Isaiah are two nine-year-old Jamaicans and
ready to talk.

Maxine: When we play games there's always people like Isaiah—they go flipping up the girls' dresses.
Adult: Isaiah you don't. . . . He does, you can tell from the look on his face.

The conversation turned to Pallavi, an Asian girl in the class.

Adult: What about Pallavi? What's she like?
Maxine: She's nice.
Adult: But they call her 'fleabag'.
Maxine: She ain't got no fleas. . .Mrs A. our Lollipop Lady, she said that Pallavi has got fleas in her hair.
Adult: Did she say that to one of the class?
Maxine: Yes, and then she started spreading it, saying 'Pallavi's got fleas in her hair'.

Isaiah was suspiciously silent during all this and it transpired later that he was a main culprit in the 'spreading' of this. Both whites and West Indians assume a lack of hygiene in Asian households, and this becomes an accepted characteristic, and perpetuated in the secondary schools. Racial tension of two months' duration involved persecution of a Cockney fourth-former of Asian origin by the West Indian element after some choice slogans had appeared on the toilet wall. A note circulating among the ring leaders said simply: 'Pakis next, O.K.?' The reason? 'They're dirty Miss, they smell of curry.' Maxine and Isaiah had no such aspersions cast on their domestic habits. But that alliance is unstable. Nick and Adam are white and Dionne and Clara are Jamaican.

Adult: If you wanted to get Dionne or Clara mad. . . .
Adam: I'd call them 'Chocolate factory'. I'd say, 'Clara invented a chocolate factory'.
Nick: Burnt in the oven.
Adult: Burnt in the oven? That's a horrible idea, isn't it?
Nick: She's white first of all and then you put her in the oven and she turns out black.

The stigma is being consciously exploited and used as a weapon. But Isaiah and Maxine, though prominent West Indians, were not taunted. Maxine was selected for interview because she was the most prolific contributor to the class discussion that had preceded. She was insistent that her names for others were a defence against those levelled at her. 'They call me them first'. Retaliation, although unmentioned by Goffman as a method of stigma management, was an almost reflexive action:

Adult: What do you think about being called 'Chocolate Drop'?
Maxine: I don't like it, but when David called me 'Chocolate Drop' I called him 'Baked Beans'.

Adult: 'Cos of his name again? If they call you a name, then you call them one back?
Maxine: Yep.

Isaiah takes it a step further. Maxine decides name-calling is because:

Maxine: They're trying to make us cross.
Isaiah: So we can chase them.

Which, according to a variety of reports, he does with alacrity. Retaliation, whether verbal or physical, was always a good policy.

The verbal retaliation revealed even more interesting aspects. It was a trend prevalent not only in Maxine and Isaiah's school. Though neither of those proved ever at a loss for words. They turned the 'burnt-in-the-oven' tables with 'Get back in your ice-cream van'. 'Chocolate drop' was counter-attacked with 'Snowflake'. This mutual name-calling was echoed in another primary school, where the research interviews were followed up in further work by their teacher. 'Blacky', 'Kojak', 'Savageman' came the way of West Indians; 'Ice-cream' allotted to certain members of the remainder, highlighted, very succinctly, the main offenders in the colour-stigma game. Those involved record their names 'Ice-cream' and 'Chocolate Drop', and the reason: ''Cos I am white', ''Cos I am coloured', etc. One, Ricky, cited significantly, ''Cos I am different to the savage men'. Both names and reasons are noticeable by their absence in the lists of the others. The nicknames, to a certain extent, both symbolise and stimulate awareness and prejudice.

This method of retaliation is again continued into secondary education, the main difference being a less poetic approach—usually 'Blacky' v 'Honky'. Not only is such a ritual interesting from the obvious awareness of difference it shows, but another intriguing phenomenon is that this particular management of stigma is completely unanticipated by Goffman—you simply *invert* the norm. Normality, all these children are insisting, is not a light, pinkish skin tone; it's a darker, tropical pigment. The abnormality, and its resultant stigma, thus is not the tan but the lack of it. Looking at school alone who could tell which group is in the ascendant in society at large?

6
The Promulgation and Enforcement of Norms

Introduction

How do people know how they are supposed to look and behave to be acceptable members of a society? To understand the dynamics of any society we must be able to answer this question. In the autonomous society of childhood and adolescence the norms of appearance and behaviour are promulgated and enforced, at least in some such societies, through nicknaming. By marking, emphasising and stigmatising the abnormal, nicknames serve to publish what is acceptable among those who promote such names and who direct their contempt upon those unfortunate enough to be their bearers.

Historical influences, of course, bear upon what is taken to be abnormal. But while the norm is implicit and has to be inferred, deviations are clearly and explicitly marked through the nicknames. We are confident that if, say, by the year 20,000 the combination of an increased noise level and genetic selection meant an earless species of humanity, the mutants still cursed with those two protuberances might be labelled 'Earwigs' or worse. Today, ears are so general, only size may differ, representing hence the infamous 'Big Ears', henchman of 'Noddy'. Nicknames *highlight* deviations from normality and, as a corollary, indicate the accepted aspects of that society. Two West Indian girls in an all-girls' school reflected on the names they had had to 'manage' at the age of nine:

> *Hyacinth*: 'Roots' was my nickname then, because of my curly hair.
> *Angela*: I did not get on with the white boys in my class and they used to call me by my colour and the second part of my surname — 'Black-head'.

Now they are 'Cindy' and 'Angie' respectively. Racial diversity is the norm in their secondary school: no stigma, no nicknames, and nothing to have to 'cope' with.

The first group of names we present derive from studies in a typical junior school. Direct discussion with the children yielded a rich crop of nicknames, usually of a pejorative character, but we were well aware that the appearance of a strange adult with some unusual interests meant that children were often only too eager to comply with requests and prove themselves to be very inventive; David J., to his surprise, might learn that 'Bones' has been a nickname of his for years though he himself might never have heard of it. Simple phonic alterations could be invented spontaneously for this interesting new adult. The very strangeness of this person, too, inevitably, would deter the more reticent children. This, of course, would be avoided by having no teacher-introduction, but the danger of an uninitiated approach could mean, too, incorrect presentation and hence indeterminate responses by the children. These qualifications to the validity of the results must obviously be made at the outset. Nevertheless, even on a contrived occasion we are recording childish creativity at work.

Still, however unsatisfactory the methods, the names gleaned were an ample illustration of the thesis: Tracy is also 'Spindle', 'Snap' and 'Wednesday'. 'I am thin and I have thin legs—"When's dey gonna snap?" — I keep getting asked.' She understands the reasons for her nicknames very well.

Body, Mind and Race

In the main social context of school three kinds of norms could be differentiated through the nicknames associated with them. The most popular type of name was that which showed awareness of physical abnormality: 'Fatty', 'Lofty', 'Freckles', 'Four Eyes' were frequent. Deviance can be made even more obvious. One nine-year-old was called, amongst other things, 'Brainchild', 'Mastermind' and 'Bookworm', but when interviewed stoutly denied his being cleverer than most. In talking to us he was with a girl classmate:

Claire: 'Brain of Britain' is more like it; Miss called him that.
Adult: You must be very clever, Nicholas. Do you feel pleased when they call you that?
Nicholas: I wish they'd shut up. I'm not particularly clever. I just read a lot of books in different subjects and they get imprinted on my brain and then when questions are asked you know the answers.

Physical and mental stigma are joined by that other renowed

abnormality—that of race or origin. The West Indian and Asian community indigenous to the area of research, because of their size and cohesion, deserve a special mention and have been dealt with in the previous chapter; but if your name is 'Denise Macmillan' you are likely to be 'Haggis'—a slight improvement on the 'Haggisbasher' she was at the age of nine—a nickname which probably incorporates name and Denise's usual reaction to that name. John O'Dea had names with a topical flavour: 'Paddy', 'Thickmick' and inversely and perversely 'Brain of Britain'.

For the nicknames of social origin, then the physical, mental and racial aspects are usually focused upon. Anything uncommon—heritage, accent, appearance, attitudes—is used as a negative identification point for that particular society.

The longevity of this stigma is based jointly on both personal and social variables. The abnormality disappears either because of personal development or acceptance by that society. Pat answers quite happily to her present names: 'Patsy' and 'Trish', in contrast to the 'Pig-nose' she was called 'by the boys at my junior school'. Adolescent girls are more sympathetic to physical peculiarities than nine-year-old boys apparently.* Julie C. lost 'Spotty' and 'Dumbo' ('I was fat') as the tense implies either by her own efforts or those of a dietician—a personal matter rather than social change. Then, of course, there is the unfortunate case of Nicola Louise G. who was subjected to 'Olive Oil', 'Tin Lizzy' and 'Matchstick'—'Because I was very thin'; and who altered neither figure nor classmates to be 'Emu' in her secondary school. 'I think I am called this as he has a long neck, and so do I.'

The stigma of socially oriented nicknames, therefore, can be localised to certain areas; while its lifespan is directly dependent on the constancy of the variables of the individual names and the social context.

Coping with a Stigmatised Identity

To shift the emphasis from the society to the conspicuous person, though it would be a little more specific about the longevity of a name —'How long do I have to live with it?'—must be a salient question to many. When does a person first become aware of this stigma and so feel he must 'cope' with it?

Jane Bundy, asked to reminisce about the various nicknames she had acquired, made the interesting comment, 'From the age of about six to eight the delights of "Bandy-Bundy", "Ginger Rusty", "Freckles" all

---

*This confirms the findings by Peevers and Secord that character becomes of greater interest than physical appearance, though not so much, we believe, among boys.

came my way. They were, without exception, the names of the playground. Shouted at me across the yard, at first my "counter-attack" was spontaneous—I disliked the names intensely.' In primary school this awareness and exploitation is unquestionable. One class was asked to compile their own personal list of nicknames for their classmates. Ronald O'B. remarks complacently in his:

'Oliver Philbert — Philpot — He doesn't like it.

Sharon George — Georgie — She doesn't like it.'

One little boy, when he was asked to give reasons for the nickname given, showed his awareness of the social stigma by answering with a remarkably cool, deliberate intent; 'Because he's ugly and peculiar.'

When visiting another primary school we noticed that Margaret A. was called 'Four Eyes' by some of the boys. When this name was read aloud to the remainder of the class, however, it was met with mutters of 'Cruel!' Two of the same class, when interviewed later, displayed the same quite acute awareness:

Adult: It's funny, isn't it? People don't like being called some nicknames. Are there some that you like, Claire? Do you like 'Fairy Cake'?

Claire: That's all right, yes.

Nick: I like Nicky, but I don't fancy Nick much.

Adult: What about all the others? Like 'Brainchild'.

Nick: I don't mind them, but I'd rather not.

Whether this awareness is exploited or not, it exists among the vast majority from a very early age, and, having been stigmatised in this way, they are unlikely to forget. But it is up to the unfortunate 'Tich', 'Taffy' or 'Dumbo' to *manage* this stigma.

The research done in this field seems to verify Goffman's theories on the topic, as cited above, though they, to a certain extent, go beyond his original three.

For example, the most common reaction to an unpleasant nickname was simply to suppress it entirely. Obviously a number of factors could be operating here, most importantly that already mentioned—the natural reluctance to admit anything as compromising to a complete stranger. Still, the effective method of carefully omitting anything with unpleasant connotations was met in every class. Claire W. was perfectly prepared to list 'Fairycake' and 'Clairy Fairy' because they had all the nice overtones the fairy world has for small girls—she 'quite liked them'. 'Spotty Dick' and 'Spotty Face' had to be supplied by the others, to her consternation. An Asian girl, Pallavi L., 'forgot' to mention 'Fleabag' and 'Stinkbomb', though a later interview revealed that her father had visited the school about the victimisation this name was part of. Clara McLeod was a very quiet girl who gave her names as 'Raincloud' and 'Cowboy', but then listen to this revealing comment by another nine-year-old:

> *Claire*: There's this girl called Clara McCleod in Mrs. B's class and every time we're playing skipping, twirling the rope around, she sometimes comes and interrupts and starts hitting. . .so we call her 'Chocolate Drop'.

Claire maintains this is a usual method should Clara interrupt, so it is unlikely Clara should forget the title, unless it is the same sort of forgetting that occurs when you have made an extremely embarrassing comment and would prefer simply to pretend the incident never existed. So, too, if you did not like your name, the easiest method was to refuse to acknowledge its existence.

Diametrically opposed to this reaction was the intrinsically positive strategy of direct retaliation. This aspect, of course, came out not in the questionnaires but in the subsequent interviews. For instance, if you are called Adam Rabbitt and dislike any variations, you can ignore them or you can hit back.

> *Adam*: You know, if they just call me 'Rabbit' I just don't go up to them and tell them to stop that. I just tell them, 'Don't call me any names, 'cos I'll call you a name.'

It must be an effective method because it is picked up by several other children as well:

> *Adult*: Do you call lots of people names? (She had supplied a great deal of information on practically everyone in the class.)
> *Maxine*: When they call me one first.
> *Adult*: I see, so you always have one ready for them? (Shakes head.) You haven't?
> *Maxine*: I have to think of one first before I call them it.

Even if you are the main instigator of nicknaming, as Maxine was, it is still predominantly a defensive reaction.

As we have described in detail in the last chapter, because of the substantial percentage of West Indians and Asians in the area, a popular jibe was 'Chocolate Drop'. It was guaranteed to produce excitement. The taunt was so common and the counter-attack of direct retaliation so automatic the response had become an accepted title for the foreign children in the school: 'Ice-cream' Maxine, Clara, etc. would reply. Retaliation was so accepted and so frequent it was an established ritual.

These two strategies to manage an unpleasant nickname, namely to suppress it entirely, or to counter-attack using the same weapons, were clearly discernible in the research material. The former, 'suppressing', seems to us a version of Goffman's 'escape' method for dealing with a stigma. But we have records of cases where the name-borne stigma has been so destructive that a child has had to literally escape and transfer to another school.

Other comments and incidents were recorded that to a certain extent substantiate the idea that other Goffmanian methods of stigma management are at work here too. The alternatives he cites are basically supporting the norm, alienating oneself from it or manipulating the stigma to one's own advantage, glorying in it so to speak. Nicholas, whose fluency and rich vocabulary we have already drawn attention to, was stigmatised for being brighter than the expectations of his fellows, and given such nicknames as 'Brainbox' and 'Mastermind'. Still, as we reported above, he ardently supported the lower standards of his fellows and wanted to be able to be seen to conform to them.

Two nine-year-olds had earned themselves the slanderous 'Fleabag'. In the face of such an offensive weapon, neither little girl could handle the situation. The following discussion ensues after we have established who is the guilty party in this nicknaming:

> *Adult*: He calls everybody names, doesn't he? I wonder why he calls you 'Fleabag' though?
> *Denise*: He started calling Denise (a friend) 'Fleabag' as well.

She shows considerable social expertise in avoiding answering a question with unpleasant implications for her by trying to implicate a friend. She broadens and so minimises the stigma she feels is attached to the word.

> *Denise*: Mum said, 'Don't take any notice'.
> *Adult*: That's the best, isn't it?

But the tone of the conversation made it clear that to be accepted and protected by the grown-up society does not make up for the policy of alienation being directed at her by her peers. Pallavi, on the other hand, encouraged isolation from the community that designated her 'Unclean'. This is an account by one of her classmates:

> *Isaiah*: I play with her. [He was trying hard to be virtuous.] We all play catching girls and Pallavi says, 'Isaiah, I'll catch some girls for you' and then I say 'All right'.

Rejected by the females of her class, Pallavi endorses and enforces this alienation by turning aggressor and ally of 'the enemy'. She, even more than Denise, adopts the first of Goffman's strategies: support the norm you are violating.

Now Adam took a different attitude. He found the consequences of having the surname 'Rabbitt' very disagreeable:

Adam: They call me names in the playground sometimes—like 'Rabbit's Teeth' and 'Furry Arms'.
Adult: Like what? Oh, 'Furry Arms', like rabbits have furry arms, so Adam should have furry arms too, is that right?
Adam: I'll have to bring a furry coat to school.
Adult: Yes, you'll have to. . . . So what do you think of all these nicknames?
Adam: I don't like them.

His dislike of this and his instinct for aggression were not sufficient to provoke a positive counter-attack. He thought he would probably try to change his nickname. 'Rabbit's Teeth' cast too great a shadow. Perhaps he, too, summed up this whole problem of living with a name. Children are aware of its power to injure, they exploit this. They refuse to acknowledge, they openly retaliate, they ignore the difference or try to change their name and presentation. The methods are numerous — but are they wholly effective? According to Adam:

Adam: 'Sticks and stones may hurt my bones, but names will never hurt me.'
Adult: That's right, so why do you dislike being called 'Rabbit's Teeth'?
Adam: 'Cos I just don't like it.
Adult: It isn't a very nice name is it, really?
Adam: I might have it changed. . .

They know the theory that asserts the ineffectiveness of names to injure — but they know that theory is false.

Senior School : Multiple Norms

The Case of 'Bog-Brush'

We turn now to a very close analysis of the social practices of a single school where elaborate and contrasting forms of norm enforcement go on through the medium of nicknaming. For the most part our attention will be focused on the social force of a single name, 'Bog-brush', and its derivatives like 'Boggoh'.

The theory that we are now advocating is based on the idea that social life is made possible only when members of a community more or less adhere to the community's norms, whether of appearance, behaviour or moral principles as used in their accounts. Often neither the norms nor the adherence given to them in the routine practices of daily life are consciously attended to as matters of reflection and policy. But the savagery of the treatment of an individual who displays any idiosyncracies that can be interpreted as amounting to differences from the accepted forms of that society suggests that deviations are experienced as in some way threatening. Since the society is numerically superior and has the benefit, as we shall show, of a power elite, an individual stands little chance of maintaining a separate stand. The method of informal control is to enshrine the idiosyncracy or deviance in a nickname handed down by that society's accepted name-giver.

We have here presented the naming mechanism in an extreme and dramatic form, purely for the sake of clarity—as if every new addition to the group were a real threat. Clearly the situation is rarely so dramatic or clear-cut. Some names are only mildly unpleasant, or even innocuous, and the willing acceptance of the name is sufficient to gain entry to the group.

For the moment, we must now examine this theory in the light of our evidence:

General Characteristics of the Results of this Study

1   Percentage response is a measure of how deeply we have sampled the school. It refers to the number of returns in proportion to the number officially on the class lists, irrespective of whether or not they were present on the occasion when the research was done. The results are presented in Table 2.

Table 2 Percentage response of forms

Form	Percentage response
3X	88
4X	95
4Y	84
4Z	76
5X	64
6X	100

2   'Name density'—It seems that the nicknaming is quite intense at the research school, and in the case of some forms, very high, although lack of standardised figures from other sources makes it impossible to be absolutely precise. Comparative figures for different ages can be seen in Table 3.

Table 3 Name density by forms

Form	Names per boy
3X	5.7
4X	4.2
4Y	7.0
4Z	5.8
5X	6.4
6X	4.6

Assuming participants give all their names

3   There are no nameless people at the research school.

Kinds of Nicknames

Analysis groups found in the detailed classification of the material were:

(i)   Names formed from personal characteristics.
(ii) Names formed as a result of particular events.
(iii) Names formed (by rhyming, alliteration, etc.) from the person's official name.
(iv) 'Traditional' names.

We have found it very difficult to be precise in the categorisation of names, especially since there is so much overlap between them. We shall discuss this matter below. In the meantime, we offer a rough guide to the distribution of name-types in Table 4.

Table 4 Distribution of name-types by form

Form classification	3X	4X	4Y	4Z	5X
(i)	41	36	72	60	50
(ii)	18	15	23	12	8
(iii)	55	22	43	17	19
(iv)	11	9	8	3	3

From the results in Tables 5 and 6, it can be seen that there is considerable overlap between the table of 'traditional' names and the table which shows the most common names, that is those names collected with respect to frequency of occurrence. We may now begin to pull out the implications of the theory which we discussed before we put forward our evidence. We had first supposed that the 'traditional' names represented definite roles, such as 'Scapegoat' and 'Joker', and implied associated and expected 'duties'. We would now wish to maintain that these so-called 'traditional' names merely represent norms which are, as it happens, held in common by many groups with a common cultural background. The traditional names are not, therefore, a separate category of 'pre-packed' social offices, though they sometimes serve as such.

Rather, the situation is that the nicknames in a given society reflect that society's prevalent norms. The most common nicknames pick out the norms which are considered by the group to be most important. Thus Table 5 is the best indicator of the pupil-society's norms in the research school, whilst Table 4 is only a generalisation of factors which are norms in many other places. The reason that the 'traditional' names recur is, as we have said, a general reflection of the norms of Western society, and therefore not very helpful when considering a particular manifestation of the same.

This theory can be checked if the themes recurring in the names in Table 5 are compared with the ethos of the pupil-society of the school (obtained by direct observation and participation). We shall not deal with this in great detail, but a glance at Tables 5, 6 and 7 should make our meaning clear.

Table 5 The 'traditional' names

Titch	Carrot-Tops	Toad
Chink	Pig(let)	Prof
Four-Eyes	Sambo	Paddy
Piggy	Fatty	Tiny
Rabbit	Slim	Shorty
Bunny-Rabbit	Smiler	Dozy
Wog	Haggis	

Table 6 Frequency of occurrence of names

Names	Frequency
Bog/Boggo/Bog-brush	10
Rabbit/Bunny-Rabbit	7
Pig/Piggy/Piglet	6
Spot/Spotty; Wog; Shit; Bog-rat/Rat	5
Toss; Puff/Pufter; Fag; Carrot; Snob; Chink	
Puss; Bender	4
Yank; Four-Eyes; Fatty; Greaser/Greasy; Sailor	
Gaffer; Titch; Eunuch	3
Vacuum; Parrot; Kojak; Dozy; Dormouse; Thunder-dick; Toff; Dildo; Haggis; Nip; Unigate; Sambo; Spunken; Squealer.	2

Table 7 Categorisation of popular names according to subject matter

Category	Frequency
Names having a reference to sex	23
Names having a reference to smoking	19
Names having a reference to race	18
Names having a reference to appearance	13
Total number of names in the sample	573
Total number of pupils in the sample	101
Average name density	5.6 names per boy

The names in Table 6 fall into four rough areas of interest:

(i)   Names having some sexual reference.
(ii)   Names referring to smoking.
(iii)   Names referring to racial differences.
(iv)   Names having some bearing on appearance.

Now let us see if there is any correlation between these names and the characteristic interests in the school.

We must begin by explaining the complex of names 'Bog/Boggo/Bog-brush'. The way the name is used is both complex and subtle:

It is applied to boys having one or both of the following characteristics:

Wiry bushy hair (like that of a lavatory brush).

Reputation for being a smoker.

Both these properties are archetypally combined in the person of a member of staff who also bears this name. From our observations, it seems probable that when the name is used, it singles out *one* of the two properties as determinative, but the association of the two properties has become so entwined that the persons so named are often not certain as to which (if not both) of the properties has earned them the name.

In a detailed study of this name in the fourth form, there seem to be definite trends in the predominance of one or other factor according to form:

4X — 'Boggo' refers only to boys with bushy hair.
4Y — 'Boggo' refers to both hair and smoking.
4Z — 'Boggo' refers almost exclusively to smoking.

When it is realised that X, Y and Z are streamed according to academic ability (and that the X form has a predominantly pro-establishment ethos, whilst the opposite is true of the Z form) then this nickname represents not only a prominent bone of contention in the school (many of the housemasters' disciplinary actions were directed to dealing with this 'problem') over the legality of smoking, but also the complex ways in which the term is used shows up the individual norms of smaller groups with respect to the subject.

'Snob' is another nickname which is common, yet confined in all its four occurrences to one form where, perhaps, in the absence of academic norms, material and social differentia are more important.

The largest group is the one containing names with some sexual reference. Some refer to prowess in certain activities, whilst others (e.g. 'Eunuch') were applied to those unfortunate individuals whose misfortune it was to remain fresh-faced and with unbroken voice for some time after the majority of their colleagues. A third division (e.g. names such as 'Puff' and 'Bender') stigmatises other areas considered to be deviations from the group norm. Conversation with pupils revealed that they were very sensitive to the public image of their type of school (i.e. boarding) with respect to the particular norm of sexual deviance.

To throw some light on the frequency of occurrence of names with a racialist bias, it is only necessary to mention that approximately 10 per cent of the pupils who took part in the research were what we describe as visibly non-Caucasoid, and these were all stigmatised with a nickname with racial overtones.

Whilst the names relating to appearances contain some fairly universal names (e.g. 'Four-eyes'), many of the names refer to aspects of appearance especially noticeable in adolescent boys: — 'Spotty', 'Pus', 'Greasy', 'Squeaker'. What is even more significant is the fact that the incidence of these names just quoted is highest at the fifth-form level, where such skin problems were most pronounced.

Thus we are presented with a Durkheimian view of each splinter group within the school. Each has its own norms which are reinforced by the use of nicknames which reflect those norms. In this sense, Durkheim could have advocated the necessity for a scapegoat, or even scapegoats, since this would encourage social cohesion by reinforcing the commonly held norms. We earlier defined the social places indicated by pejorative nicknames as 'slots'. We can now see that these traditional slots are real, though they are not absolute. The evidence we have will only allow us to say that the names reflect the norms, and some norms are more generally prevalent than others. Whether there are some sort of Jungian archetypal names we find it impossible to say.

Certainly there is a whole continuous spectrum in the degree to which a name isolates an aspect of a society's norms — it is this process of 'coming to heel' on the part of the individual that reinforces the norms. The scapegoating role is not usually a separate and absolute office, but just a selection of people exhibiting a higher degree of deviancy from the norms.

Two pupils in particular were singled out for community abuse, but the 'scapegoating' taking place here did not appear to *confine* the derision to these two. Rather, these two individuals transgressed to a higher degree more of the norms of the pupil society than their colleagues.

In the research school nobody avoided receiving a nickname. It would seem reasonable to suppose that in this context, where pupils are forced into a situation of close proximity, there is no alternative but to become integrated into the society. Those who cannot fit in (and we know of a case to support this) find life so unpleasant that leaving the school is the only course available.

The Relation between an Individual, his Nickname and Dominant Groups

We have thus far dealt with naming as a method of norm-reinforcement. This is to look at the subject from the point of view of the *society* in question. We now propose to examine the question from the point of view of the prospective entrant or member of that society. We have argued that the individual's individualism is a potential threat to the group's cohesion. The group asserts its normative influence in the form of a name. We now want to argue the next step, which is that the individual's acceptance of the society, and his acceptance by that society, depends on how he manages this nickname. The nickname is a symbol—a very powerful symbol of his identity as viewed by the group. The more the individual deviates from the group norms, the worse is the stigma, and thus the harder to accept.

At this point we may also throw in the question of whether nicknames are purely descriptive, or whether they are actually *prescriptive* as well. We would wish to argue that the answer is not as straightforward as one might expect. The name is descriptive in so far as it singles out for comment something peculiar to the individual, but it must be remembered that this idiosyncrasy is labelled by the group, and is therefore only relative to that group's norms. Thus each name is a definition with respect to group norms. So there is an element of prescription in naming, purely through the logic of the case. Whether there are any empirical grounds for people acting out the implications of their names is another matter. What evidence we have so far suggests that, in general, names are both suffered and acted out.

It is clearly difficult to obtain direct evidence to support the thesis that what we may call 'social competence' is very much tied up with the management of a nickname. The only absolutely objective way would be somehow to be able to observe pupils interacting informally, then record their dialogues and actions and assess their degree of social integration. This would then be followed by their re-living their lives, but somehow managing their nicknames differently the second time round. The two results could then be compared. Clearly such a procedure would be impossible.

If we *assume*, however, that an unsatisfactory relationship with the group will produce in the individual a selection of emotional responses such as feelings of unhappiness, rejection or aggression (a not unreasonable assumption), then it will be possible to study the relationship between an individual's satisfaction with his nickname and his degree of acceptance into the group.

We also hope to show (in the manner of Hargreaves, 1967) that each form has a clique structure, and that it is the dominant clique in the form which determines the dominant norms, and to which, to some extent, all members of the form have to defer.

Table 8 'Dominance league'

4X Names	Points	4Z Names	Points
α	18	A	22
β	14	B	13
γ	13	C	10
δ	8	D	9
ϵ	7	E	5
ζ	5	F	5
η	3	G	2
θ	2	H	1
ς	2	I	0
κ	0	J	0
λ	−1	K	0
μ	−3	L	0
ν	−3	M	0
o	−3	N	0
π	−5	O	−1
ρ	−5	P	−1
σ	−5	Q	−2
υ	−7	R	−2
ϕ	−8	S	−3
χ	−9	T	−6
ψ	−10	U	−10
ω	−12	V	−18
		W	−23

The list represents the form arranged in order of dominance, with names being substituted by letters: Greek letters in the case of 4X and Roman type for 4Z.

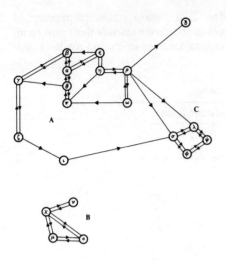

Figure 9 Sociogram of 4X

Table 9 'Clique' hierarchy order

4X	Group A	Average dominance	8.3
	Group B	Average dominance	14.0
	Group C	Average dominance	18.5
4Z	Group A	Average dominance	5.7
	Group B	Average dominance	8.0
	Group C	Average dominance	10.0
	Group D	Average dominance	13.0
	Group E	Average dominance	16.0
	Group F	Average dominance	18.5

'Average dominance', as explained in the text, is merely a way of adding up all the integers of the group members' dominance numbers, and then finding the average for the clique. The 'dominance number' itself is merely a convenient way of putting the form in an order after analysis of questionnaire returns, so that the most dominant person in the form has a number of 1 and the least dominant are in the twenties. Thus the group with the highest dominance actually has the *smallest* number.

The sociograms which appear in Figures 9 and 10 do not show the relationships which members of the form have with other people outside the form under study. The Table below shows the number of choices made by the participants in the survey *outside* their own form, and this is placed alongside the total number of choices made in each form.

Table 10 Relations outside the form

Form	Outside the form	Inside the form	%
4X	24	70	34
4Z	44	80	52

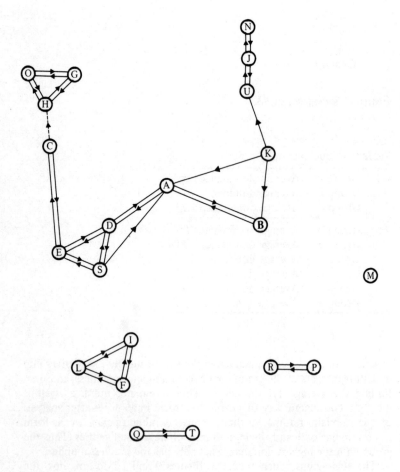

Figure 10 Sociogram of 4Z

Table 11 Reactions to nicknames*

	Group	Response	% of 'c'
4Z	A	5 @ a; 2 @ b; 1 @ c	12
	B	3 @ a	—
	C	3 @ a; 1 @ c	25
	D	1 @ a; 2 @ c	60
	E	1 @ b; 2 @ c	60
	F	1 @ a; 1 @ b; 1 @ c	30
4X	A	6 @ a; 5 @ b; 5 @ c	30
	B	3 @ a; 2 @ b; 1 @ c	16
	C	3 @ a; 2 @ c	40

'a', 'b' and 'c' represent respectively the responses to questions asked on the questionnaire.

(a) means that the subject has no strong feelings about his nickname.
(b) means that the subject rather likes his nicknames.
(c) means that the subject wishes that he didn't have the name.

The column of percentages shows that there is a general trend towards being unhappy with the status quo as we move *down* the group hierarchy.

Table 12 Reactions to the form (i.e. the class as a social group)

Form	Group	Reaction
4X	A	11 @ a
	B	2 @ a; 2 @ b
	C	1 @ a; 1 @ b; 2 @ c
4Z	A	4 @ a; 1 @ b; 1 @ c
	B	2 @ a; 1 @ c
	C	2 @ b; 1 @ c
	D	1 @ b; 2 @ c
	E	1 @ a; 1 @ c
	F	1 @ b; 1 @ c

For the sake of brevity, we have put the attitude information into a coded form.

The participants were asked what they thought of their form as a group of social people. We have sorted the replies given to this question into three groups, which are as follows:

*See also separate section on pupil reactions to nicknames

(a) a positive and favourable reaction to the form.
(b) a neutral or non-committal reaction.
(c) an unhappy or hostile reaction to the form.

In Table 8 we have attempted to give straightforward linear expression to the order of dominance of personalities in each form. The participants in the survey were asked to name the people in the form who took a leading role in any activities, and after that they were asked to list the people in the form who were manifestly without any leadership role. The two sets of data have been conflated to produce the lists in Table 8.

The sociograms in Figures 9 and 10 were produced by analysis of the data gathered from asking participants the following question:

'I want you to write down the names of the people you go around
with most at school. Please do *not* write down more than five
names. If you mainly go around with just two people, then just
write down those names. . . .'

We have substituted Greek letters for the names of boys in 4X, and Roman capital letters for the names of boys in 4Z.

If we put together the results in Table 8 and the sociograms in Figures 9 and 10, it is possible to see who the dominant cliques within each form are. Table 9 shows this dominance hierarchy. We have suggested that the dominant clique in each form would lay down the norms which dominated the form. The results we now have can help us to assess the worth of this assertion. We thus examine the ethos of these two forms, as a test of the theory, to see if there is any correlation between the form ethos and the ethos of the dominant clique. Our treatment will be brief since we are here only looking for the general trends.

4X
The sociogram in Figure 9 shows that this form is composed of three main groups:

(i)   Group A, both the largest and the most dominant group.
(ii) Group B, consisting in only four members.
(iii) Group C, again of four people.

In addition to the above, there is also a pupil who appears to have no relationships with anyone in the form.

The 'X' form is the stream with highest ability in the fourth form. Despite this, the atmosphere in the form as a whole was not noticeably well disposed towards academic study, although there are a small number of boys who seem to maintain a genuine academic interest outside the classroom. The prevalent attitude was one of slight indifference to work, although the work was usually produced. The attitude was certainly not one of quiet intellectual keenness.

This brief sketch of the form is both supported and explained by Figure 9. The three central members of Group A a, β, γ are also the three highest dominance figures in the form, and their group contains the majority of high dominance people in the form.

The boys a, β, and γ, as well as other members of Group A, show a fairly cool attitude to work, the prevalent philosophy being to do (or at least *appear* to do) the bare minimum to get through. There was also a fair amount of interest in sport, and a general dislike of members of Groups B and C.

Group B was markedly more academically able in general than Group A, with half of its members having school academic awards. It shares music, electronics and sailing as interests in common.

Group C was also of higher academic ability than Group A, and the ethos of this clique was that of the intellectual—it was members of this group that would stay behind after lessons.

4Z

The picture in this form is not so straightforward. Whereas in 4X only one clique had no connections with any other, here most groups are totally isolated from one another. Group A is the almost archetypal collection of schoolboy vice: smoking, illicit meetings with the opposite sex; opposed to academic study; rough, etc. This atmosphere pervades the form, and 4Z have a reputation for being what might be described wryly as 'lively', and 'playful'.

Group B consists in only three members, all of fairly high dominance. These people are more clownish than Group A, and have fewer brushes with authority.

Group C is made up of boys who are not only in the same house but also share the same study. It is tenuously connected to Group A via Group A's outermost member, who shares the same study as those in Group C. This group is much quieter in temperament and does not indulge in smoking, etc., and if any group in the form could be considered to be academic, then this is it.

The remainder of the form is split into three pairs and three total isolates.

As we have mentioned above, clique A's norms dominate the form. Thus the 'academic' form turns out to be rather cool in its attitude to work despite the intellectual quality of many of its members. The lower stream form has an ethos of roughness and vice, despite the quiet and isolated nature of the majority of its members. In both these test cases, the character of the form and its norms seems to be determined, then, by the dominant minority. These norms are reflected in the spread of interests in the nicknaming (cf. p. 78 ff.)

Individual Reactions to Nicknames

It remains to be discussed now how the nicknaming system 'feels' to its inmates, since most of the discussion so far has been either from the theoretical or social angle. What does having a nickname mean to the average pupil of secondary-school age? Perhaps more important (at least as far as the individual is concerned) is what can be done about the management of a public identity which a nickname might mar. As Goffman has said, 'Shame becomes a central possibility arising from the individual's perception of one of his own attributes as a defiling thing to possess and one he can readily see himself as not possessing. . .' Management of a disagreeable identity waits upon the realisation that the identity is actually *undesirable*. The techniques for dealing with identity management are many and various. As has been said before, living in a society consists in sacrificing individuality to community. The optimum is to achieve maximum social cohesion with the minimum sacrifice of individuality. How far this balance is obtained, and in what ways, must be left to the pupils themselves to say.

If less than half of the population have at some time had some cause for dissatisfaction with the names with which they were born, and this is considered only a minority dissatisfaction, then the same cannot be said for people's reaction to their nicknames.

An average of around 70 per cent of the people interviewed reported a positive dislike of at least one of their nicknames. A further average of 9 per cent were at least ambivalent about them—which leaves only 21 per cent who were quite happy about their nicknames.

We will let the people speak for themselves. Why is it that nicknames can raise this amount of feeling?

Living in any society involves at least some sacrifice of individuality. Without this there would be anarchy. The security of belonging to the group is bought at the price of the individual personality. In the end it is a fine balance—the individual must not have to pay more than he receives in return. Nicknames are the group's way of presenting to the individual aspects of the group norms as they most personally affect him. He is called upon to fit into the norm, to come to heel. This would seem to be why the names often hurt:

'I hate it. It is stupid. . . .'
'. . .makes me feel bloody stupid. . .'

Compare the reserved

'I dislike them and wish them not referred to. . . .'

with the suppressed indignation of

'People think that small people are always speaking in high voices (for reasons you can probably imagine). I think it is very juvenile. . . .'

And

> ' "Tim" is the only nickname that I have that I feel fine about. What I hate are names like "Fatty" and "Tubby"—anyone who calls me that is treated to a scream of rage and a blow in the face. . .'

For others the nickname is too embarrassing to mention:

> 'The one that will not be repeated is the only one I do not like and would love to change it. . .'

Others choose to invalidate the name by invalidating the giver:

> ' "Skinny"—Well I don't get called it much and the people who do are not worth bothering about. . .'

The reactions of people to their nicknames in this manner might suggest that there is a conflict going on between how the individual sees himself and how his group sees him—a conflict between self-image and persona as perceived by society:

> 'Embarrassing. Makes me feel threatened mentally. Some do not present a true image, i.e. who wants to be described as something they are not. . . .?'

> 'I dislike nicknames because people use them to imply your character. . .'

> 'I do not like being called "Water rat" because it specifies what I am meant to look like. I also dislike "Scruff" because the name continued after my hair was cut. . .'

> 'They made a complete mockery of my good taste in dress. . .'

> 'I want to change my name when I have been feeling rotten with life. . .'

Some people do not stop at simply being unhappy with their nicknames — they take the offensive:

> 'One I quite like, the other I detest. The only person who uses it *regularly* has had an equally stupid name invented by me. . .'

Others take a rather more quietist view, wishing

> 'simply to drop most of them. . .'

In the end, most begin to come to terms with their names, even if in fairly halting and conditional terms:

> 'I don't want to have any nickname, really, but if it is nothing cruel or nasty about me, I won't really mind about it. . .'

'If they are hurtful, then I don't mind. . .'

'I couldn't really care about my present nickname, but I might care if it was changed to something silly. . .'

Some begin to recognise the group significance of having a nickname:

'And I do not dislike them because everyone has got a nickname and so you are not different from the others. . .'

And,

'I think I really don't mind it—everyone has nicknames they dislike and I am one of the group. . .'

'I like being called nicknames as it sounds casual and friendly. . .'

Confirmation of this picture comes from another detailed study in a different kind of school in another part of the country. Of sixty-eight people interviewed, thirty-eight said they had been pleased to be given a nickname and twenty-one that they had been displeased, while nine had held changing or ambiguous attitudes towards their nicknames.

The Influence of Nicknames upon Behaviour

If people do perceive pejorative nicknames as highlighting socially un-desirable characteristics, and they themselves subscribe to that norm-ative system, it seems likely that getting such a nickname could lead to actual changes in physical appearance, where that can be managed, and to the suppression of old habits and quirks of behaviour held repre-hensibly deviant by the dominant group.

In a subordinate study we discussed with people the idea that nick-names, in stereotyping, may 'fix' a character, or otherwise influence behaviour. People showed that they were well aware of ways in which a nickname might directly affect a person's behaviour. Somebody whose nickname highlighted his being underweight related that he had tried, unsuccessfully, to put on weight, while people whose nicknames re-ferred to overweight had similarly attempted to lose weight in response to the having of the nickname. One person averred that she would literally fight anyone who called her 'Fatty' to her face. A very clear example of a nickname directly influencing behaviour was of a name applied to a boy at the age of eleven, on moving to grammar school. This was 'Farmer', a mocking reference to his apparent Oxfordshire accent. The name did not last long since he quickly learnt to modify his speech to the norm required.

Another reply described an interesting example of the way in which nicknames may function, that is by stereotyping the image of a person within the minds of the group to such an extent that the character of that person is stifled. She comments 'I became associated with a certain role, which was difficult to shake off later, when the nickname continued to be used.' Perhaps, surprisingly, this nickname was of the name-derived type.

Not less important, in terms of self-image, and behaviour, is the group acceptance of a person, commonly reflected in the bestowal of a nickname. Several respondents in the study referred to this, commenting variously that the name gave them confidence, helped them to feel at home in the group, and that

'It was very pleasant to have a name which I felt I had in some way earned or merited, as opposed to ones that you are given at birth.'

Different Kinds of Schools

The public boarding school and the state day school are, at least from the casual outsider's point of view, totally different sorts of institutions. We discussed this rather more fully above, where we examined the significance of the fact that the tendency in many day schools that we have looked at is for there to be a percentage of pupils (generally somewhere around 20 per cent) who manage to avoid a name. However, we have found one particular form at least in a state day school where no one escapes the naming process, but the signs are that this is the exception rather than the rule. We shall discuss this particular occurrence below, but first we must make an attempt to sketch in general terms the main features of the naming systems in both state and public education and note their similarities and their differences. When we have done that we shall be in a position to try and assess possible reasons for the differences. We propose to concentrate the contrasting description under three heads: name density; the named/unnamed boundary; class or cultural traits in the names.

Name Density

By this we mean, in simple terms, the average number of names which each pupil has. This is easily calculated by adding together the total number of nicknames in the group and dividing this total by the number of people in the group. Clearly, this is a fairly rough and ready sort of measurement, but it is sufficient for our purposes to show convincingly what the relevant trends are.

If we select a state day school and a public boarding school, we find that there is a marked difference in the naming densities. The range in the boarding school varies between 4.2 names per boy to somewhere around 7.0 names per boy. Compared with this, the day school offers the great bulk of averages at around 1.0 – some well below this. Even the highest average was under 2.0. This difference is striking – the *highest* name density in the day school is not even *half* of the lowest name density in the boarding school.

The Named / Un-named Boundary

All we can say at this point is that the trend is for there to be on average approximately 20 per cent of the day-school class who manage to avoid receiving any nickname at all, when nicknaming is a prevalent social practice. In the American secondary school, as we have seen, nicknaming is largely absent, yet in the boarding school, without exception, no one escapes the naming system.

We have found at least one form in a day school which could claim to have a name for everybody in the form. As this could be an important border-line case we shall examine the matter a little further. We must bear in mind the context of the information; the school is for day pupils only. Each class is assigned to a form master, and the form has a single particular room in the school which it calls its 'form room', where it spends some of the time when lessons are not in progress. It is in this room that such administrative tasks as 'taking the register' are performed. This is in contrast to the boarding school, where the house system predominates and much of the administration takes place in the houses in which the boys live. In this situation, classrooms are reserved almost exclusively for teaching purposes, and it is the houses which act as meeting-places and social centres. Let us set down some of the comments made by members of the day-school form under question, about themselves:

> 'We're mad. . . Immature. . . we do things as a form more than anyone else in the school; we stay together as a form at break-times and lunch-times.'

> 'Very conscientious; academically good; intelligent – although occasionally rather "playful".'

The form members claim to have inflicted various damages on their form room, and to have a rather active social life. This seems to include a game called the 'Arena Club' where the desks are arranged in a circle and a member of the form is put in the middle whilst the surrounding desks gradually close in and crush the unfortunate in the centre. Other 'rainy day' diversions involve what they call 'Torture'. This involves removing the victim's shirt and holding him over the room heater. The victim tended always to be the same person in practice, although I am assured by the victim himself that this was not really unpleasant. All are equally adamant that 'Torture' is a game that is no longer played.

There are three or four boys in the form who do not fit in. They seem to avoid going into the room at break-times and lunch-times. Other boys describe them in words such as these:

'They're very quiet — they won't mix. They don't stay in the room at break.'

'They are quiet, weak and often taunted.'

'They're shy — they don't mix. They don't get on. One of them is not quite all there.'

There are about four people in the form who act as ring-leaders. None of these characters will initiate action on his own, but when they get together things can get started.

From this description it would be very easy to run away with an over-dramatised picture of both the form and the school to which they belong—madness; human-baiting; torture; blood sports. Clearly, much of this is a projected public image. This particular form are, in general, intelligent, and some of those we interviewed were 'gentlemen of impeccable manners', despite their covert claim to a liking for human blood.

Compare this with the form with the name density of 4.2 in the boarding school. This is how the pupils see themselves:

'The form is very mixed in character — big-mouths; snobs; quiet people; good people and bad people. It does have a high academic standard.'

'Not bad — the odd moron here and there. Generally good blokes.'

'Twenty-two people — wild, lively, noisy, intelligent.'

'This is a good form, but there are certain members of the form (not mentioning any names) who are extremely juvenile and take every inch they can get. Also, if you can believe it, some people smoke in lessons.'

'Load of perverts. Very good at finding two meanings to words. Very sociable — with spastics.'

This form is of a similar age and academic ability to the day-school form. From the quotations it will be apparent that we are dealing with approximately the same sort of animal—quite intelligent, boisterous, with a few people in either case that do not fit in. Again, in either case, there is a similar fairly closely knit atmosphere which holds the form together. The difference is that this *esprit de corps* is exceptional at the day school, but rather the rule at the boarding school. The day school has a high social cohesion compared with the other forms in the same day school, whereas the form we have examined in the boarding school is not exceptional at all when compared with other forms in the same school. It is, we would contend, the high degree of social cohesion that enables proper definition of the group to take place, and it is from the group that the nicknames spring. Both these forms have established their ethos so widely that no one is able to escape contact of some sort with the group. The degree of interaction means that no one, similarly, escapes getting a nickname. That the boarding school situation is more intense is shown by the far higher name density. Both, however, are intense enough to allow no one to escape their naming system or group structure. This is not the case in the less cohesive forms in the day school, and this is sufficient to explain the existence of a number of pupils who remain un-named.

Class and Cultural Differences

It is now time to look at the actual subject matter of the names that occur, to see if we can detect any signs of class difference. The romantic might perhaps expect the public-school name system to be rich in references (albeit oblique) to a distinguishable way of life, characteristic of the 'upper classes'. We can say that he will be disappointed. As far as we can see, there certainly are *some* differences, but not in this direction at all.

For the sake of uniformity, we shall continue to use the same two forms to provide the illustrative material but they are, so far as our evidence goes, quite typical. Below we shall discuss the distribution of subject matter of names more thoroughly, so until then we shall satisfy ourselves with summaries. To add a little flesh to what might otherwise be something of a skeleton, we give some examples of actual nicknames. It must be remembered that in the case of the boarding-school form, the number of nicknames used per person is over *four* times as great as the number in use in the day school.

We can categorise the boarding-school names according to subject matter roughly as follows:

(i)   Names having some sort of sexual reference—statistically clearly top of the list (32 per cent).

(ii)   Names having a reference to smoking (26 per cent).

(iii)   Names having some reference to racial characteristics (24 per cent).

— both (ii) and (iii) are equal in their popularity.
(iv)   Names having reference to physical appearance (18 per cent).

Table 13 Specimen names from boarding-school form

Bender	Spotto	Thunderdick
Haggis	Guffy	Peter Perfect
Chink	Rabbit	Loony
Hulk	Biceps	Bleep
Snob	Bog	Humphrey
Nip	Joe 90	
Wert	Gas fart	

Table 14 Specimen names from day-school form

Elvis	Chips	Stav
Tab	Halo	Hoover
Chin	Basil	Dun
Denis	Rabbit	Piccolo
Ruby	Flipper	Bob
Ernie	Cheeko	
Noddy	Stan	

In the case of the day-school names, the position is very different. The smallest group in boarding school (group (iv) names having some reference to appearance), is by far the largest in day school, often varying from 50 to 75 per cent. In the case of the particular form in question, well *over* 75 per cent of the names are derived from the details of personal appearance. Another 20 per cent are accounted for by names derived from official names. What is even more striking is that all references to sex, race and smoking are absent.

There are visibly non-Caucasoid people in the form and neither is smoking a bone of contention as it is in the boarding school. That is not to say that no one at the day school smokes—they do. However, if you happen to be a confirmed tobacco enthusiast at a day school, and the powers-that-be are not, you can always wait until you get home (or if you're desperate, a discreet 'drag' on the way home). If you live in a boarding-school 'home-time' comes only six times a year. The enthusiast is forced to take more drastic and dangerous measures.

The differences in the role that sexual matters play in the sources of nicknames is intriguing. Both schools are single-sex, all-male preserves. One can only assume that the finer points of adolescent maturation are not the topics for general discussion that they are at the boarding school. This would fit in with the difference between an environment which is a place for work only (and for comparatively short periods), and one which provides for work, all meals as well as sleep.

Thus there is a quite considerable difference between the nick-naming in these two sorts of institution, but the differences seem to correlate with the degree to which the institution corresponds with Goffman's model of a 'total institution' (i.e. the duration, proximity and intensity of social control) rather than to any class or regional differences. On this point some of the pupils themselves put forward their own sobering thoughts. One observed that a couple of people in the form came from homes where there had been marital break-down 'but we never mention those sorts of family problems'. Children who do make a show of wealth are liable to find themselves called something like 'snob'. Child society does not have the values of the commercial adult world.

Conclusions

Nicknaming is clearly closely involved with the social norms of the pupil society. Furthermore, it seems most likely that the social norms in each case are those of the dominant clique within each form. As we have argued, we believe that the nicknames that occur do not fall into cut and dried categories, but rather reflect (so far as we can see, with a fair degree of exactitude) the norms of the dominant clique. The spectrum of the nicknames is wide, as is their pejorative content.

Second, an examination of the evidence supports the thesis that social dominance is the key factor in the establishment of norms and, hence, the sorts of nicknames given. The evidence for this is, in our view, most striking. The evidence correlates a positive attitude to the form, an acceptance of one's nickname and one's place in the clique hierarchy in a very positive way. As far as we can see, the evidence would suggest that nicknaming and social competence are connected in a general sort of way, rather than that the management of one's nickname is determinative of one's social competence.

Hargreaves (1967) reports that in his research school, 20–40 per cent of relationships were taking place outside the form structure. As Table 10 shows, the figure at our research school is much higher—some-where between 35–50 per cent—perhaps even higher than that. This fact is easily explained by the nature of the school. Our research school was a boarding school, with a strong house system. Indeed, the signs are that relationships within houses are at least as important as those within forms. The pre-eminence of the form as a social unit is further weakened by the fact that only a few lessons per week actually take place as form lessons. For the majority of the week, pupils are in sets.

Nevertheless, this finding does not weaken the thesis that the dominant group in the form sets the form norms.

Reference to Tables 11 and 12 presents us with information regarding pupil attitudes with respect to their nicknames and their form. A glance at the result shows that there is a positive correlation of satisfaction with form and nickname with the pupil's position in the form's clique hierarchy. It cannot be too strongly emphasised that that is only a general trend. There are considerable individual differences.

It is interesting to note that the *total* outcasts in each form seem unconcerned with their positions. Dissatisfaction is more common as the social ladder is descended—but dissatisfaction itself seems to presuppose that the pupil concerned is actually *on* the ladder, whereas this is not so for the outcasts.

7

The Practical Uses of Insult

In the preceding chapters we have had occasion to notice the use that nicknames are put to as inciters of rage, as weapons with which to tease and irritate people. In the following piece of fiction we have as good an example as real life can provide of the introduction of the nickname into the unfolding of a challenging conversational form.

Joby and Snap, out for an evening loiter, come across the neighbourhood bully, Gus Wilson:
'How do, Gus.'
'Now then, Joby. Where you off to?'
'Oh, nowhere. Where are you going?'
'Same place. I see you've got Copperknob with you. Ey, Copperknob, made any good lies up lately?'
'What's up with you?' Snap said. . .
'Has your uncle shot any more planes lately?' Gus said.
'I never said that', Snap said.
'Garn, you did. You said he'd shot down three planes in Spain.'
'I never did say that.'
'Are you calling me a liar, Gingernut?'
'You're calling me one.'
'That's different.'

The Name Game

Nicknames, we have stated, differ from their official counterparts in two main aspects: they are labels attached in the course of existence, rather than at its outset, and they are usually bestowed by peers in a variety of *informal* social situations.

Translating this into school terms means they are the names of the playground, the walk home, the teacherless classroom. Nicholas comments:

> *Adult*: Does Mark (an inveterate name-caller) use them to you in class? Would he say ' "Brainchild" can I borrow a pencil?' or something?
>
> *Nicholas*: At play-time sometimes, when we are staying in to do a job for Miss, or sometimes if we are doing an assembly, if we have got permission to stay in and get on with our lines, sometimes he'll do it then.
>
> *Adult*: I see. Does he play chase or something in the playground and call people these nicknames to get them to chase him?
>
> *Nicholas*: No. We usually play football and he calls lots of people names there. If he wants people to chase him he'll ask them.

Think back to your own schooling—that playground. . . a whirl of skirts and grubby knickers, muddy shoes and socks, groups of 'Mothers and Fathers', games of 'Off ground tig', handstands, and always at least one person wailing with injured knees. Nicknames are part of this world. Jane Bundy, as we quoted earlier, recalls her first encounter with the phenomenon: 'But Jane wasn't enough for the social jungle of the school. From the age of about six the delights of "Bandy-Bundy", "Ginger", "Rusty" and "Freckles" all came my way. Without exception these were the names of the playground, shouted at me across the yard. . .'

Children realise from a very early age, in their first quarrels, despite the 'sticks and stones' rhyme, that names can hurt. Your opponent's face crumples, he or she turns and runs howling to Mum. That warm feeling of victory imprints the potential of name-calling into a child's brain.

The lesson is learnt early and never forgotten. Nicknames are deliberately used as weapons in the playground. Weapons, too, are both defensive and offensive.

> *Adult*: What about you Maxine? They call you 'Chocolate Drop', don't they? Are they being nice, or trying to make you cross?
>
> *Maxine*: They're trying to make us cross so we can chase them.
>
> *Adult*: And what about Isaiah? Oh, do they call you 'Blacky' and 'Kojak'? Do you mind?
>
> *Isaiah*: I chase them.

Isaiah, particularly, used names as a way of beginning a good game of chase, and it was an acknowledged procedure. Listen to Nicholas on the possibility of starting a game in this manner:

> *Nicholas*: No, I wouldn't—if you get caught, then you'll get walloped, because if you ask someone (instead) then if you do get caught you don't get hit, but if you call them names and that, if you finally get caught, then you get walloped.

Though he rejected it on prudential grounds, he considered it a viable alternative to the more explicit request.

Nicknaming has become an integral part of children's antagonism in the playground to such an extent it often forms the prelude to some games, so much so it has become a sort of ritual—the word used, in fact, in Jane Bundy's account:

> 'they [nicknames] usually formed the prelude to an enjoyable game of "Chase" or even "Fighting" for my taunter. The names were used as offensive weapons to annoy and they invariably did. At first my counter-attack was spontaneous—I disliked the names intensely,—but gradually they became the tacitly accepted ritual before "Chase".'

As animals use a carefully stylised succession pattern of moves as a preamble to formal combat, so nicknames can provide the verbal prelude to open physical hostility amongst children. Denise W., as we have already noted in a previous section, was 'Fleabag' to most of her peers and, if she failed to 'rise' to the various names and comments coming her way, had her hair pulled. Adam, who was unlucky enough to be Adam Rabitt, disliked the resultant titles of 'Furry Arms' and 'Rabbit's Teeth' to such an extent that he was contemplating changing his surname. We have given the actual quotation in a previous section.

'Sticks and stones' don't actually 'break bones'—true, but they often serve as a prelude to something equally violent, or are powerful enough in themselves to hurt when used as small, vicious, missiles, carefully aimed and deliberately thrown.

Retaliation

In the middle of a vitriolic argument the natural form of address seems to be the surname, or some nasty descriptive nickname, and perhaps a form of intermediary power is the use of both first and surname together. An incident among eight-year-olds ran as follows:

> *Simon* to Julie, who is trying to take away a hose pipe: 'Stop it, stop it.'
> *Gloria* in defence of Simon: 'Look here *Fatso*.'
> *Simon*: '*Julie Pearce*.'
> *Julie*: 'I can't help it, I'm too strong.'

Annabel to Simon: 'Can I say something to you?'
Simon: 'Sit down.'
Julie: 'I can't [sit down].'
Simon: 'You can't have a go then. You can't speak properly.' Julie
grabs the pipe from Annabel.
Simon to Annabel: 'Shut up, she [Julie] had it first.'
(Simon appeals to the convention that the firstcomer has priority, but
in fact Annabel had it first.)

Later, in a game of football:

Simon: 'Owen is a kicker, Owen is a fouler.'
Gloria: 'Four Eyes' [He does indeed wear spectacles].

Jimmie knocks over Andrew while he is running.

Jimmie: 'You blumming twit.'
Andrew: 'Pig.'

(Jimmie is indeed an exceptionally fat boy and easily the fattest in
the school.)

Nicola calls across the playground: 'Jimmie fatso.' Jimmie ignores
this.

Operative Epithets – How to be Chased

Merely repeating a child's name over and over again may be all that is
necessary to cause him to chase the speaker. In addition, the name may
be followed by 'try and catch me' or a more provocative utterance like,
'Armadle it, the big fat shit', 'Armad, he's mad, he's mad', 'Jason's
getting eggy, Jason's getting eggy', where the word 'eggy' is an Oxford
word meaning that somebody is getting angry and about to attack
somebody else. An operative epithet is an insulting descriptive phrase
having the force of a pejorative nickname, but only of transmitting use
and significance.

Five girls (Alison, Nicola, Sarah, Susan, Katie) to Gordon: 'Cheese
face, cheese face.'
Nicola: 'Chase us.'
Gordon: 'I'm not going to chase you.'
The girls: 'Gordon, Gordon, dirty face.'
Alison: 'White hair, Gordon is a dirty face, Old Granny Faddock.'
(Gordon does have very blond hair.)

All the girls poke at him. Gordon hides behind a nearby wall, then reveals his presence and starts to chase them. On catching Alison, the two pretend fight and disengage.

> *Alison*: 'Old Granny Faddock.' And swipes at him with a paper hanky.
> *The girls shout*: 'The boys are getting eggy, the boys are getting eggy.'
> *Alison*: 'Gordon, Gordon, Gordon.'
>   Gordon goes off, Katie follows him. He turns round to say: 'Not playing.' He tells the girls: 'I don't want Katie to play, I don't need her to play.'
> *Alison*: 'Only Zeena can play, he only wants Zeena.'
> *Nicola*: 'Do you want Rachael?'
> *Gordon*: 'Rachael – yeh.'
>   The girls use their toilets as a safe retreat and try to get Gordon to chase them.
> *Gordon*: 'I'm not playing, go on, clear off.'
>   Play-time ends.*

This episode incorporates many of the aspects already mentioned. In order to try to get Gordon to chase them, the girls start off with a somewhat innocuous operative epithet 'cheese face' and progress to phrases based more on his personal appearance, 'white face, dirty face', ending up with his official nickname 'Old Granny Faddock', which, of course, he cannot let pass. Gordon proves to be quite aware of the power he has to choose whether or not to participate in the chasing, even to the extent of dictating which girls he lets tease him. At a more general level, it may well be the case that the activity of teasing can be viewed as having certain well-established rules, and it would be the task of future research to establish what these are and how children learn them.

It is not only in England that operative epithets are used as missiles to throw at people to either annoy, hurt, or simply initiate some type of game.

From Spain it is reported that during the course of a month-long English course run by the Jesuit Order and using English assistants the pupils, varying in age from eight to thirteen, regularly used mild insults in a mixture of English and Spanish to provoke the English teachers into giving chase or some sort of mock battle. Terms of abuse included such things as:

'You are very donkey' (From the idiomatic Spanish, *'Eres muyo burro*).

'You are very tonto' (stupid).

*We owe these incident descriptions to A. Sluckin.

'Chorizo.' (A subtle term of abuse. Its root meaning is 'a long Continental type of sausage', but it has acquired overtones somewhere between our English 'You silly sausage' and 'You great prick'.)

After the insults had been dished out, the English teachers were expected to give chase.

Achieving Character by Verbal Hazard

Why do some people do unnecessarily dangerous and reckless things? Mountaineering, gliding, gambling and the like? Goffman has seen these activities as occurring in bounded times and places, in generalised public view, in the course of which 'character' is built up by the display of courage, coolness, competence and a certain largeness of being. In the gambling saloons of Nevada one has the bathetic end of a spectrum at the other end of which are the glories of the conquest of Everest.

Children, too, look for occasions for 'action' in which they can display and achieve 'character' and some of these occasions involve potent words. Two obvious categories of potent words whose public utterance takes nerve are secret names, such as teachers' first names or nicknames, and swear words. Both are used by the children of Oxfordshire in achieving character. These devices can best be illustrated by quoting the observers' original anecdotes.

> I taught a fourth-year class. They all knew my Christian name but did not use it. There was in the class a group of lazy and not very clever girls. [Later discussion with this participant observer revealed that the group in question were at the top of the social status ranking within the class, and thus the incident can be seen as part of their continuing testing and maintenance of their positions.] One day one of them called for attention while they were doing some writing, by saying 'Kevin!'. I looked over, acknowledging that I had heard, but giving neither a negative nor a positive emotional response. Further, I went over to help only when I had seen some people with prior claims. Thus in one way status was *not* gained because I treated being called by my Christian name no differently from being called 'Sir'. However, status may have been gained in the group because I could hear by the tone of voice that it took some courage to call out 'Kevin'. This was definitely not a set-up traditional game.

An interesting point about this incident is Kevin's cool response to the hazard. It might seem as if the teacher has to be seen to be provoked, that is, there has to be the risk of punishment or anger before the hazarding would really work in the building of character. That this is not so is confirmed by an anecdote from another school. The participant observer reports that 'the younger pupils, however, some-times played a kind of game, by deliberately calling me by my first name in the presence of another teacher, to see how both she and I would react'. On this particular occasion the teacher did not acknow-ledge this, although she undoubtedly 'overheard'. Clearly the numbing non-acknowledgment by the more experienced teacher nipped the hazard in the bud, though as our first informant remarks, some charac-ter would be achieved by the mere fact of the utterance of the potent word, whether or not it provoked a response.

Oxfordshire seems to be the home of another word-hazard, in which forbidden words are publicly uttered. In the words of the informant:

> One such device which I did not encounter personally, but of which I have heard of two examples, is 'shit-shouting'. If a lesson were getting particularly boring one boy would whisper 'Shit'. It was then up to a boy in the vicinity to repeat the expression in a slightly louder voice, and so on. The winner was he who said the word loudest without provoking the question, 'Who was that?' from the master in charge.

As with much of social life, in hazarding, too, symbolic actions may replace the playing with dangerous words. Thus we have a penumbra at the end of speech forms in which a suitable action in a special scene becomes endowed with potency in an intermediate realm still far short of the kind of 'real' action found in mountaineering or sailing.

8
Names as Character Sketches

In this section of the book we shall look at nicknames as possible indicators of the development of the preconceptions of others, that seem to be present in most people's way of describing others. We shall try to estimate their value in this regard by analysing the kinds of noticings of others they have stemmed from.

The relationship between naming or describing and perception (and action) has been the subject of a long-running discussion, initiated notably by L. Vygotsky and B.L. Whorff. Whorff began his professional career in the insurance business. While he was investigating fire risks an explosion occurred because of the careless throwing of a match into a 'pond' at a factory. No fire precautions had been taken to minimise the hazard as the liquid was designated a 'pond' and, therefore, he concluded, treated by everyone as non-inflammable. Unfortunately, in this instance, the 'pond' was a solution of highly explosive gaseous waste matter and thus extremely dangerous. The incident was one of several that exemplified to Whorff the significance of language, particularly names and labels, in codifying personal experience, the label, thus, being symbolic of the conception and determining it. We might go on to suppose that people, too, are treated in accordance with the names they are given.

Vygotsky (1962) would argue this even more strongly. He maintained that language is a method of structuring personal experience internally and, as the articulated manifestation of this structure, can act as the initial symbol of the mental processes and, as it were, determine prejudice in advance. Thus we can grasp what is the attitude of one person to another by studying how he talks to and of him, and in particular by paying attention to the names, titles and nicknames he uses.

The symbols used with the most specific intention of categorising people are surely nicknames. A person is named or renamed in the light of the attitude and conceptions of others to him in many cases.

Consequently, nicknames can, in one sense, be seen as the external manifestation of the concepts of others of that individual, their implications, their biases, their limitations. To a certain extent, too, they can be interpreted as indicative of the conceptual level of those employing the name. Other factors obviously complicate this simple relationship between the user and the object of that name. Other factors complicate the process of tracing back from the symbol to the nascent concepts. The degree of personal involvement between the parties always falsifies the result a little, though nicknames here have the counter-balance of quite a widely disseminated usage. The personal aspect is, thus, minimised. They are more indicative of a general consensus of opinion about that person and his character.

Having examined the basis for linking nicknames with cognitive processes by which persons are categorised, let us now turn our attention to the level of sophistication of the categories. Is it possible to deduce anything about the development of person-categories and the bases of the judgment of others?

This topic—how children think of other people—has been the subject of a recent study by Peevers and Secord (1974). A very brief summary of their conclusions will provide us with a basis on which to compare the results from nickname analysis.

Their research was conducted with pupils of the 3rd, 7th, and 11th grades at high school and finally at college, and took the form of a person-to-person interview, the children being asked to describe people known to them. These descriptions were recorded and the terms and contents analysed in an attempt to formulate a theory about the development of personal concepts in children. The results showed that stable characteristics were attributed to both self and peers quite extensively. Situational behaviour was the method of differentiation employed most consistently. These conclusions were drawn by elucidating the balance of descriptive concepts of various kinds within the content. This gave 'a measure of the extent to which the observer differentiates the observed person from himself or from the situation in which he is known'. To assess the amount of 'descriptiveness' four type categories were devised:

1   Undifferentiating items were those conveying little or no information about an individual as such, e.g. his possessions, family or location. The preponderence of this kind of category was inversely proportional to age.
2   Simple differentiating items were those that made a clear distinction between the person and his setting or possessions, e.g. physical characteristics, single acts, global statements ('He's nice'), whether the person was liked or disliked, within which broad social groupings the individual came, etc. This group of categories is diffuse and common in

personal descriptions at all levels.

3 Differentiating items gave fairly specific personal characteristics: interests, beliefs, activities, feelings. The referents are thus less concrete and more specific than previous categories and are apparent only in the descriptions offered by the later ages interviewed.

4 Dispositional assessments involve the attribution of 'traits', i.e. reactions and attitudes that have validity for that person in a variety of situations. Again they are much more commonly used in the latter two age-groups.

The results suggest that the allocation of descriptions in each category differed substantially enough to constitute a definite progression in the development of concepts for describing persons, the undifferentiating or simple differentiating being replaced by items that demanded a more complex, sophisticated assessment. People, concluded Peevers and Secord, are registered initially only as types and are only vaguely differentiated from contexts and situations. Then, gradually, out of these amorphous feelings and impressions, sharper distinctions develop. The child learns to crystallise the person as a single entity, separate from his environment. His perceptions are increasingly nicely differentiated because of his accumulated personal experience and reference ability, and people gradually assume abstract qualities, unique, in degree at least, to themselves as individuals.

Both the other and the self-descriptions collected reflect this trend. At an early age, the child is totally unreflective; then the ability to describe 'play' activities emerges. At the age of nine, particularly in girls, interest in physical appearance evolves; trait characteristics begin to contribute; while the very final stage is the capacity to delineate oneself in terms of abstract projects—aims, ambitions, etc. Implicit in this is the progression from concrete, global items to a more abstract, nicely differentiated formulation of specific dispositions.

This development from the general to the specific is paralleled in several other fields: M.M. Lewis (1969) in describing the acquisition of language, Goffman in analysing methods of speedy personal assessment in interactions and Vygotsky, in tracing the development of language and thought, have all noted this progression from general, undifferentiated reference to greater perception of detail and idiosyncrasy.

The question now is whether nicknames in their function as condensed personal descriptions substantiate or contradict this idea of the development of personal concepts. To assess the conceptual implications behind a nickname, to try to establish the concepts that are implicitly formulated in them, we must go back to the basic premises they stem from. What are the main sources or referents in inventing our nicknames for others? Are they the echoes of a slanging match, overheard at break-time? Do they highlight some idiosyncrasy of physique or character? Are they simply mutations of the official name, with no personal referent value at all?

For the purposes of this chapter we introduce more material in a deliberately contrived variation of conditions, both to see whether there are regional variations in the relative descriptive content of nicknames, and to test whether, as personal descriptions, nicknames exhibit the content progression with age discovered by Peevers and Secord in their classical study of how young people describe each other.

To make the results generally acceptable and applicable, the surveys were carried out in two contrasting areas, one being predominantly rural, the other a rapidly developing urban centre. In both areas nine- and thirteen-year-olds were focused upon; the reason for these age choices will be explained later. The names collected were categorised on the following principles:

1   Those based on the recognition of some physical abnormality, e.g. 'Fatty', 'Four Eyes', 'Lanky', etc. (These were abundant).
2   Those based on the recognition of some mental or behavioural differentiating characteristic: 'Brainbox', 'Jumbo', 'Nutcase', etc.
3   Those based on the recognition of a verbal analogy with either the first or second name, the members of this rather broad category being anything from the very simple mutations 'Susan'–'Susie'; 'Jones'–'Jonesy', to the more complex processes involved in 'Keith'–'Keef'–'Beef'–'Beefbroth'–'Broff'.
4   Those based on the knowledge of some biographical event of the person—either in a name used in school, or picked up from home—as e.g. Louise became 'Boo' because a little sister could not pronounce her proper name; or based on some shared biographical incident in class, etc.—one thirteen-year-old became 'Becky' after the class had read *Tom Sawyer*.
5   Those based on a simple traditional association: 'Nobby Clark', etc.

The results of both surveys can be tabulated below, as percentages:

Table 15 Percentage of nickname origins

Area	Age	Physical	Personal	Verbal	Biographical	Traditional
Rural	9	35	9	51	3	2
	13	26	12	50	8	4
Urban	9	38	8	54	0	0
	13	29	14	43	9	5

As the table indicates, the percentages between the areas show a remarkable similarity and, given the difference in region, suggests that the proportions apparent might well be valid for the majority of nickname origins. Having noted this cohesion of distribution, the next most striking aspect of the results must be the vast number of nicknames derived from their official counterparts. The preponderence is slightly distorted, however, by the number of simple syllabic mutations contained within the figures. 'Rodge'—'Roger', 'Rob'—'Robert' contribute to 33 per cent and 43 per cent of the names within this category. The mutation is so traditional or slight that their claim to the status of a genuine nickname is uncertain, without a close parallel social study to discover their force. The large number of names that have been manipulated on this purely linguistic basis does seem to suggest, however, an interesting parallel with the stage in language acquisition outlined by M.M. Lewis (1969), the 'babbling' stage when a baby, perhaps because of a pure enjoyment of sound and utterance, articulates continually. Meaning, in this stage, is of little or no importance. The parallel is strengthened by observations during research. One of the hazards of the methods adopted, as we have noted in previous sections, was the tendency of the children to be over-enthusiastic. Compiling the nicknames of an individual with the help of the class often, therefore, meant the risk of lots of ingenious names being invented on the spot. The names that arose out of a situation like this were interesting in the enormous number of very simple phonic rhymes or alliterations that were volunteered. Celia Johnson, for example, cited her nicknames as 'Seal' and 'Four Eyes'; the class, eager to be helpful, chorused 'Johnny', 'Sea-lion' and 'Johnson's Baby Powder' almost all in one breath. The responses were simple and based on the original name alone. These cannot be entirely ignored since the direction of syllabic mutation may be influenced by perception of character, so that one of the variants produced by 'babbling' may stick for an external motivation.

By way of confirmation of character-encapsulation of nicknames we cite the following passage from the autobiographical *Cider with Rosie,* by Laurie Lee. *Cider with Rosie* is the account of a small boy growing up and discovering the pleasures and the pains of life in a small Cotswold village. By the age of five his attention is attracted by the colourful characters it contains:

'Cabbage-Stump Charlie' was our local bruiser—a violent, gaitered, gaunt-faced pigman, who lived only for his sows and fighting. He would set out each evening, armed with his cabbage stalk, ready to strike down the first man he saw. . .he would take up his stand outside the pub, swing his great stump around his head, and say 'Wham! Bash!' like a boy in a comic, and challenge all comers to a battle.

'Albert-the-Devil' is another unsavoury character stigmatised in personality and habits;

a deaf-mute beggar with a black beetle's body, short legs and a mouth like a puppet's. He had soft-boiled eyes of unusual power which filled every soul with disquiet. It was said he could ruin a girl with a glance and take the manhood away from a man, or scramble your brains, turn bacon green, and affect other domestic disorders.

Albert's character, it seems, is accurately encapsulated in the nickname he is given. The practice of nicknaming for character was widespread in the village.

Among others I remember [says Laurie Lee] was Tusker Tom, who sold sacks of tree roots for burning. And Harelip Harry, Davis the Drag, Fisty Fill, and the Prospect Smiler. The first three were orbiting tramps, but the last was a maniac farmer. Few men I think can have been as unfortunate as he; for on the one hand he was a melancholic with a loathing for mankind; on the other, some paralysis had twisted his mouth into a permanent and radiant smile. So everyone he met, being warmed by his smile, would shout him a happy greeting. And beaming on them with his sunny face, he would curse them all to hell.

We are now in a position to compare the nickname system with Peevers and Secord's results. For instance, the 'non-differentiating items', it can be seen, correspond most closely to the biographical names:

| Andrew B. | Farmer | Lives on a farm |
| Keith K. | Yank | Nationality |

These names convey the minimal specific information about the most general category to which a person belongs. The Peevers and Second results must be partially masked by the social control aspects of the naming process. Language is a method of publicising the conditions for social cohesion. Any verbal interaction within a group can only be meaningful when, explicitly or implicitly, common terms of reference are established; otherwise group relationships break down. A group can exploit this phenomenon by establishing its peculiar terms and labels. To function as part of this clique one has to 'break' the code—comprehend and utilise the referents—often to acquire one oneself. Thus the ritual of nicknaming is often an initiation rite, at the primary stages of acquaintance, when only cursory, vague concepts of character have been assimilated. These non-differentiated names, thus, are a permanent but minimal feature of the social order, because they are frequently superseded by others of more specific content.

The 'simple-differentiating' items are found mainly in those nicknames that are physically derived. Both focus upon outward appearances without reference to imperceptible abstractions such as dispositions.

Of the names evolving from some sort of personal premise, that is physical, personal, biographical, between 75 per cent and 80 per cent in both age-groups and areas are taken from this category. Such a number certainly substantiates the Peevers and Secord claim that they play 'an important part in personal description throughout'.

Meanwhile, the 'differentiating' and 'dispositional' items correspond to those names stemming from perception of social roles or personal attributes.

Phillip D.   Cass   Because he is tough

seems to account for that little boy's behaviour in the required 'wide range of situations'.

Janice O.   Calculator   I think I have earned this nickname because I am fairly quick at working out
mathematical sums

focuses on a specific ability, that is both abstract and particular in Peevers and Secord's terms. The difference here is not so much quantitative as qualitative.

The younger ones were able to perceive and codify a close relationship:

Camilla   Plum   Goes with Lucy
Lucy   Pudding   Goes with Camilla

a neat method of verbalising a relatively obvious social phenomenon.

Pete   Big Pete   Keeps his hands in his pockets

Such a nickname is an implicit recognition of the Goffman theory of social performances. If one assumes identities and adopts performances with respect to particular situations, it implies a 'core identity'. The phrase is Arthur Brittan's (1973). It is the motivating force behind these negotiable, projected, temporary names. Peter G., putting his hands in his pockets, is analysed by his peer group into the component parts of this 'core identity', that is they conceived of the performance – the actual performance – by making the assumption of social ease and superiority behind such a confident pose. 'Big Pete' is a rather disarming indication of an extremely fine perception of abstract notions in social interaction and apprehension of motive and character. Both the American study and the nickname surveys tally in finding the appearance of this variety of name (or description) only in the later ages.

Certain aspects of the initial research have, therefore, been validated by the subsequent analysis of nicknames: undifferentiated and biographical details are minimal. There is a marked preponderance of simple-differentiating items and physically derived names, the criteria for both being similar. Only in the advanced stages is there evidence of any sophisticated social perception. In fact the correlation would appear to be close enough to prompt further, more intensive research into this area.

The comparison of results of the two age-groups has validated the progression and the main aspects of this trend with regard to the Peevers and Secord theory. Both sets of figures indicate a difference in naming between the ages, but it is the difference of gradual change rather than the disparity of a decisive break. During adolescence conception both of self and of others undergoes considerable change. This apparently cataclysmic transition is, however, apparently unreflected by the various personal labels attached. If nicknames are indeed to justify our claims to their being the surface manifestations of deeper psychological processes, then why aren't these tremendous personality changes of adolescence also reflected? The explanation must, we think, lie in the multiplicity of factors contributing to any nickname. We have linked it, true, to thought patterns and the individual's attempts to structure his world. Goffman's theories about social stigma also show a similarity to nicknames too strong to be ignored. They are closely linked, then, to minority and prejudice in a given society and perhaps even dependent on them. They are subject to that uncontrollable variable of the individual—his physical, mental, biographical idiosyncrasies, and how adequately he copes with them. All these—the psychological, the social, the personal—are variables directly affecting the constant—the nickname. Any change in one of these aspects, thus, for instance the personality changes of adolescence, can either be accentuated or counteracted by the other two forces exerting their influences on the situation. Unless these also remain constant, very little alteration would be apparent.

Another aspect of nicknaming, however, became discernible in the course of research. Again, a definite progression could be traced when comparing the two lists of nine- and thirteen-year-olds. The change this time, however, was not in the content of the name itself but in the actual process of name-giving. We noted previously that the great majority of nicknames were internal formations—between 55 per cent and 60 per cent of the entire total. Of this number, in turn, particularly with the younger age-group, these took the form of very simple, sometimes spontaneous syllabic mutations; 'Nicholas-Ridiculous' etc. This variety of verbal experiment was likened to the 'babbling' stage with babies—both being purely phonic explorations for the sheer joy of articulation, meaning being largely superfluous. Just as the 'babbling' is a transitory phase in the acquisition of language, so the tendency among children to respond solely to the aural quality of a name was, in the later survey, superseded by a reaction to meaning, so that a far more complex thought pattern was apparent in the actual naming process. Having noticed this phenomenon, the names were analysed again, this time focusing upon the method, rather than the content or origin of the name. Results were as follows:

Process	9-yr olds	13-yr olds
Simple mutation	77%	57%
Pun/irony	8%	15%
Analogy	15%	28%

For these figures to be meaningful obviously an explanation of the categories is essential: Simple mutation entails, as explicated above, merely a slight alteration of the name, usually the addition of a suffix: Bundy-Bundy-o/Bundo; a direct rhyme: Jill-Pill; or simple and often meaningless mutation: Nigel-Niggles, etc. This category, as the table illustrates, is prevalent in the nine-year age-group, but is gradually absorbed into the two others. Pun/irony involves a more complicated and intellectual manipulation of the name, though the response is still predominantly to the phonic rather than the semantic content. Nine-year-olds were capable of the letter play of:

Sarah Tibbets   Stebbit   Titbits

But there is only one notable example of a name undergoing a triple process:

Vincent Parsloe   Lieut. Parslow   Lieut. Pidgeon   Loot

whereas, in the twelve-to-fourteen age-group, this is a far more common occurrence:

Jackie Amos	Amosquito	Flea
Steven Hill	Chill	Charlie
Joanne R.	Josy	Dozy
Richard Cantwell	Tin Cantwell	Tin
Tracy F.	Wednesday	'When's dey gonna break' (Thin legs)

Puns, too, involve a response to meaning rather than the sound of words:

David Sharp	Acker	Latin equivalent
Martin Southcott	Eastbed	Antithesis of compounds
Andrew Barefield	Barefield Sobers	Pun and allusion

In the thirteen-year-old selection, too, the nicknames are often ironic:

John O'Derr   Brain of Britain   'Cos he's a thick Mick really

This category reveals a far more complicated and sophisticated manipulation of the original name, and a tendency to respond not to the sound of the word but to its meaning. The numbers in the group almost double in the latter survey, suggesting a far more complex thought process emerges proportionately with age.

The third category—that of the allusive names—shows evidence of the children reaching into the realms of their entire experience to supply the name. Again the group demonstrates a remarkable increase at the later stage. The nine-year-olds tended to simply add the 'type' names: 'Fatty', 'Lanky', 'Brainbox', 'Four Eyes'. The thirteen-year-olds, on the other hand, use everyday experience as referents far more frequently. The 'Tubby's of the primary school have become the 'Cannon's and the 'Chubby Chequer's of the high-school comprehensive. The analogy can be triggered off by either appearance or actual name:

Debra Brown	Henry	Like that dog on TV
Heather Taylor	Tiger	Like that girl on the 'Double Deckers'
Jane Percy	Percy Thrower	
	Percy Parrot	Reasons apparent
	Persil Automatic	
Sharon Gonsuales	Speedy	Speedy Gonzales
Judy Lancaster	Bomber	Lancaster Bomber

The trend is, we think, worth particular attention because, to a certain extent, it reinforces an aspect of the Peevers and Secord report. The 'Tubby's' etc. of the earlier group do seem to imply the process of a type concept being applied, without any significant modification, to individuals. And this validates the American account of the initial method of applying simple 'global' referents to personal concepts.

The marked increase in the allusive content of names, too, implies the process of naming by continual reference to personal experience of the environment. The 'type' figure is individualised by finding parallel examples in their world—the mass media playing, perhaps, a significant role. This would substantiate tentatively claims about the actual process of differentiation in personal concepts, increasing contact with the environment (directly proportionate to age) shading in the details, helping to discriminate more finely, improving perception and making others, in fact, three-dimensional.

9
Name-Givers

Who gives the nicknames? The various social forces and personal emotions unleashed by the use of nicknames are sufficiently potent, we hope to have shown, to suggest that the role of name-giver is a position of considerable social influence and perhaps even of power. Sometimes we have reason to think one, and only one, individual has been responsible for the entire eke-nomenclature of his classmates and other associates. In one case we have recorded, one boy has successfully nicknamed over forty others. In one private junior (prep) school we studied, hardly any nicknames were invented and promoted by pupils, indeed they hardly used nicknames in this particular school, but those that were in use were exclusively invented by the headmaster, alone amongst the staff. There is, it seems, considerable variability as to who the name-giver is, but it is clear that whoever he or she may be it is a role of power.

Faithful to the idiographic, intensive method, we turn now to an exposition in detail of some particular cases, to illustrate the types of name-giver we have noticed.

Individuals as Name-Givers

Nicknaming, we have established, carries with it, inevitably, a certain amount of stigma. It very often highlights abnormalities and idiosyncrasies in a given society. It also, on a smaller scale, delineates individual differences in attitudes. The boy that yells 'Cowardy Custard' after a retreating pair of heels is showing his awareness of the value of physical bravery (or the lack of it) in the playground. It may simply not have any importance to his neighbour.

In several of the different 'societies', the classes that were studied, it became obvious that just as certain roles were always occupied: the

Leader, the Toughie, the Joker, etc., so, in a few, one person took on the role of the Name-giver. This elite set of the schoolyard society seem to fit a carefully designed niche.

Quite frequently the roles of leader and namer are synonymous. Of the children who took part in the primary-school survey, those selected for individual interviews were often those who had been a fount of information. Peter W. and Isaiah P. are two notables who merit attention. In both cases their list of names for others was endless. Although both took care to cover any tracks, a very similar picture emerged. Isaiah, we discover, really enjoyed his play-time, happily employed in 'flipping the girls' dresses' and leading games of Chase. His classmates put his Chase into context for us: Denise (to us, 'Fleabag' to the others), states that the first person to give her her unwanted title was not the Lollipop lady—as Isaiah and his friend had intimated—but Isaiah P. himself. He also 'started calling Denise "Fleabag" as well.' Isaiah, it appeared, relished a game of Chase and had discovered that the best method of acquiring 'chasers' was to antagonise, either by name-calling or by dress-flipping.

Isaiah, then, used names with a very specific purpose: to unify the people in his 'gang' and simultaneously, and more importantly, to provoke and alienate others.

Peter W. used the same technique and the same setting—the anarchy of the playground—but whereas Isaiah's main aim was to infuriate and lend realism to Chase, Peter's seemed to be a basic and very clear-cut division in his class and to rally peers specifically around two poles. He was mentioned by his teacher as one of the main elements in name-calling that went on out of the classroom and a more careful scrutiny of his list revealed that he, along with two others, acknowledged themselves to be 'Ice-creams'. Several coloured children, on the other hand, described themselves as 'Blackies, Nig-nogs, Enochs', etc. Peter and his friends were obviously asserting the normality and correctness of their pigmentation and ridiculing the others, who retaliated with the opposite theory. Peter was attempting on a small scale to amplify perceptions of racial difference. He can be allotted the role of name-giver, rather than his cronies, as a result of the illuminating comments of his peers. Both are dark-skinned, but react differently to him; one, Steven S., describes him in his personal list quite categorically as a 'Fatty', and 'Long-haired Monster'. The hostility beneath is perhaps because Steve has suffered in the all-too-painful-present at Peter's hands. Ali K., as we have already noted in a different context, escapes the 'Blacky'-hurling, the mild 'Ali Baba' and 'Shorty' being the nastiest names to come his way. A quick glance at the sociometric graph plotted by the teacher provides the explanation. Ali is a mate of Peter's and therefore enjoys the peace of political friendship. Peter uses his role as name-caller to segregate as firmly as possible the 'Ice-creams' from the 'Enochs'.

Teachers as Name-Givers

The third namer of any significance is not a pupil, but a 'Miss'. Asked to fill in very simple answers about their names, nicknames, and the reasons for them as far as they knew, one cause kept cropping up: 'Miss calls me that'. The follow-up touched briefly on this point (quoted *verbatim* before) and revealed that at least five of her class had been named by her in various situations. They may not have been the main ones the class knew that person by. However, they were still in acknowledged, if only occasional, usage. Here the name-giver has a far more sophisticated awareness of the power of names—they are not used, as in Isaiah's case, simply to provoke; or in Peter's to segregate; here they are used to enforce the relationship with her class. She labels and categorises certain members, the others take up the cry and they have, simultaneously, adopted her system of values, her definition of normality and idiosyncrasy, if only temporarily.

One primary school, too, threw up another consideration. In this the headmaster was kind enough to allow the entire nine-year-old population to be questioned. This meant that three classes could be surveyed and the results compared. Examining the various answers showed, to a certain extent, the classes were distinguishable not by the linguistic technique involved but by who was name-giver, teacher or child. Perhaps the easiest way to illustrate this is to look at the most extreme example, a class where the teacher was the only name-giver.

Adult: Miss X calls people by their nicknames a lot doesn't she? How many has she in all?

Nicholas: About five I think.

Adult: There's David Bellamy, who's Bellamy on the Botany. . .

Claire: Yes. And she calls me 'Claire de Lune'. Nicholas was Nicholas Ridiculous.

Nicholas: Margaret T. is sometimes called 'Marguerita'.

Adult: And wasn't there one who is always called 'Sleepy Drawers'— Miss X gave him that because he's always dropping off to sleep?

Nicholas: Sometimes when Miss is calling the register she'll say 'Robert A', 'Robert A?'—again no answer and in the end you have to give him sharp nudges.

In this case the teacher in question was a very competent and experienced lady, with a very clear idea of class control, who inevitably stamped her personality on the class, which echoed her names as a result. Nicknames can often act as a barometer of the social climate within a classroom — here the wind prevails in a teacherly direction.

In this case where we are certain that a teacher, and it is a powerful teacher who does it, has given the name, we were hoping for a more elaborated naming technique to emerge—but in fact even the most powerful and inventive teachers use the same system as the children. We illustrate this with some examples.

1 Internal motivation: 'The Whale' from 'Jonah' from 'Jones'.

2 External motivation:

(i) Physical characteristics deviant from an implicit norm. 'Mary Ann' and 'Mary' were names given by teachers, at a school for the subnormal, to male pupils who had certain feminine behaviour traits. These names seemed to be in wide circulation amongst the children themselves. (We think we should add, in case anyone should feel moral outrage welling up at this point, that so far as we could see there was no deliberately malicious intent on the part of the teachers in their distribution of names. Just like the children, by highlighting a deviance they were promulgating and enforcing norms.)

(ii) Biographical incident: 'Carrots'. The master began drawing a carrot on the blackboard. A boy who had not been paying attention was asked what it was. He was told it was a carrot, and from then on the master used the word as a nickname for this boy, a very typical incident. In no time the other boys had picked it up. This is a school where nicknaming is a flourishing institution.

This incident prompts the general question of how much teachers use nicknames for their pupils. Sampling a wide variety of single-sex boarding schools, it seems clear that only very powerful teachers can and do use them. Is this a reflection of those teachers' power, or a part of it? We are still unclear even as to whether this question is well conceived. It may be that as a teacher's power and reputation grows so does his capacity to promulgate nicknames and his confidence in giving them. This growing capacity enhances his power and so on. We would need to follow a teacher's career in very great detail to find the answer to this question, a project which in all likelihood could not actually be carried out. In the school for the sub-normal, to which we have already referred, the teachers nearly all regularly use nicknames both to refer to and to address the boys. It seems clear that felt power and the confidence that goes with felt power and the sense that one can freely use nicknames are closely connected. In these cases they represent the common inversion in which a large social difference is marked by an asymmetrical use of terms of address which ordinarily are used for relations of the closest intimacy. The same inversion has been noticed by Brown in his examination of the changing use of the two pronoun system in French, where 'tu' is used both between intimates and asymmetrically to indicate great social distance, as an aristocratic diner might address a waiter or a taxi-driver, in the old France at the turn of the century.

Dominant Clique as Name-Givers

We have just seen some examples of particular individuals in the group acting as name-givers for the whole group. For the outside observer, as well as for the member of the group, it is often very difficult to recall who in the group is the accredited name-giver, since one of the marks of a successful name-giver is that his names somehow seem to fit naturally into the ethos of the group so naturally that their author is often forgotten. Moreover, we have seen examples of other individuals who have been unsuccessful in inaugurating a change in their own name, or wishing an unwanted name on anyone else.

We want to suggest that there are reasons for these phenomena. We believe that particular individuals are able to act as name-givers to the group because of their place high in the group's hierarchy, and since, as we have established, the names which are given tend to reflect the norms of the dominant clique in the group or form, the name-givers become the arbiters of taste and morals. That the dominant clique in any group has a marked effect on the ethos of that group has also been shown in other respects by Hargreaves. By examining the sort of subject material which nicknames pick out we have seen that there is a correlation between the group norms and the norms of the dominant clique within that group.

We would expect that if the nicknaming system was, in part, a desire for broadcasting the norm of the dominant clique they would control that system, and emerge as the most successful name-givers.

The final stage in our examination is to see how the dominant clique influence and control the distribution of these names.

In a detailed study* of the entire fourth form of the research school with respect to the single name-complex 'Bog/Boggo, etc.' we found the following results:

4X — 'Boggo' refers only to boys with bushy hair.
4Y — 'Boggo' seems to refer equally to both hair and smoking.
4Z — 'Boggo' refers almost exclusively to smoking.

There is a trend of decreasing pro-school attitude from 4X, through 4Y to 4Z. This trend is reflected in the dominant clique's attitude, both in all our researches, as well as those of Hargreaves. In the case of 4Z, the dominant people in the form are notorious for their illicit smoking. This is not the case with their opposite numbers in 4X. This difference in the interests of the dominant clique is reflected in the way the nickname 'Boggo' is used.

---

*Fully described in Chapter 6.

10
Nicknaming in Other Cultures

The material reported so far in this study is derived from systematic studies in Britain and the United States, societies closely linked historically and arguably part of the same cultural complex. To test the universality of our idea that there is an autonomous children's world with its own moral system and standards of appearance and conduct, and that nicknaming as a social practice is a prime device by which it is recreated generation by generation, we must examine in some detail the nicknaming practices of other societies, particularly those that are both part of literate culture with a complex and differentiated social system and very different from our own. Japan and Arabia seem the most obvious candidates, since a study in Africa, if conducted in urban surroundings, would reflect in all probability the dominant European culture, while village life is likely to be insufficiently complex to allow an autonomous children's world to become sharply differentiated.

Japan

Informants on Japanese linguistic customs including the use made of contractions and nicknames emphasise, in their social commentary, that such nominative formations are not very much used, since their use would run counter to Japanese ideas about formality and politeness. Yet, on further discussion, it is surprising to find that there is indeed a submerged culture of nicknaming, with, it strikes us, a distinctively Japanese flavour.

Official dislike of the use of nicknames is reflected in the fact that nicknaming is currently prohibited in most Japanese schools. This is explained by our informants as part of the ordinary insistence on politeness between people. Private schools are actually able to achieve almost complete prohibition of nicknames since classes are large and school days are busy, competitive and lack any serious intimacy. At the most a kind of affectionate abbreviation of the surname or personal name is allowed. Thus for classifying Japanese naming practices we shall distinguish contractions much more sharply from nicknames than we would in classifying the practices of a Western culture, such as that of Spain and its former colonies. We shall notice that even the affectionate abbreviations have a semi-polite character, making use of title suffixes. Since there is a great variety of state schools, differing in academic and social standing, there are some where there is no effective prohibition of nicknames, and then they do occur. It has been suggested by one of our informants that before the post-war population expansion schools were smaller and more intimate and there was much more use of nicknames. We have checked this hypothesis among older Japanese and it does indeed seem to be the case.

Our study of English nicknaming practices suggested that one of the most powerful effects of nicknaming was the promulgation and enforcement of social norms, by a kind of internal control, exercised within the tight-knit society where such naming practices flourished. In Japan social control and the promulgation of norms seems to be much more an external matter, particularly in the way social norms from the adult world are imposed directly upon quite young children, in such matters as the giving of respect to older persons. In these circumstances there seems little room for spontaneous methods since there is much less, so we gather from our informants, of the independent social world of childhood than amongst Western children.

The Formation of Contractions

These are used to mark intimacy and as a sign of affectionate regard. They fall into two groups.

(a) Those derived from surnames, which are used as markers among adults and classmates. For example 'Ishikawa' yields 'Ishi'. More interesting and we think very illuminating as to Japanese social conceptions is the contraction from, for example, 'Ikeda' to 'Ike-san' where 'san' is an honorific title, roughly corresponding to Mr or Mrs. We are assured by our informants that there is none of the trace of irony such a use of a standard title would carry with it amongst Westerners.

(b) Among family and friends a contraction from first-names serves the purpose of a marker of intimacy. For instance 'Yumiko' ('-ko' being the traditional female suffix) yields 'Yumi-chan'. This is a formation of the greatest social interest since 'chan' is a suffix specifically reserved for young children, but it is not a diminutive in the European sense such as '-kin' or '-ly'. It is the title used formally for or to a young child, corresponding, we understand, to the obsolete 'Master' and 'Miss' of traditional British usage.

Nicknames Proper

Our informants emphasise that nowadays these are used only amongst lower- and middle-class children before they go on to high school.* According to our informants they survive into adulthood only in the lower classes. We have not been able to make any cross-check on this hypothesis. It is clear that they are formed on a much narrower etymological basis than that employed in the West. There are basically two methods of formation:

Physical characteristics

(i) Direct descriptive name. For example, 'Chibi' for someone small and cute, 'Debu' for chubby, 'Noppo' for tall, 'Hage' for bald, 'Megane' which simply means 'spectacles' for a child who wears them, it being comparatively unusual for children to wear them. Like the corresponding nicknames these seem to mark out deviations from the Japanese 'Mark I Standard' Child.

(ii) Animal and insect associations: these include 'Zo' (elephant) for someone larger than normal, 'Bear-chan' for someone chubby and cute with large eyes, 'Kamakiri' (Mantis) and 'Batta' (grasshopper) for thin children, 'Tombo' (dragonfly) for someone with protruding eyes.

(iii) Other object associations. The name 'Geta' (wooden shoe) is used for someone with a square face.

Personality and social behaviour
Again, there are several sub-categories.

(i) The names of historical or folk heroes are adapted to this use. There are, for example, 'Genji' for a playboy, 'Hide oshe' for one who works hard to rise in the world, and 'Ninomiya kinjirod' for a bookworm. Only one of these, 'Genji', is definitely pejorative.

(ii) There are several directly descriptive words used as nicknames, such as 'Noroma' for slow and lazy people, 'Tono' for someone who is bossy. Sometimes 'Sensei' (teacher) is used for the same type of person, 'Meijin' is used for someone who is expert at doing things, but not in a pejorative sense. It corresponds to the English 'Prof' rather than any version of 'Know-all'. 'Gacha-ko' for a chatty girl, seems to be based upon onomatapoeia.

---

*We have some doubts about this claim. An experienced business man who worked in Japan for many years informs us that his staff called him the 'big white polar bear'.

(iii) Finally, there are names formed by association with animals and with things. 'Mon-chan' (from the English word 'monkey') for a tomboy; 'Kearu-chan' (frog) someone idle, cute and with a wide mouth; 'Dump' (from the English 'dump-truck') for someone big and aggressive.

It is apparent that if this is a representative sample of Japanese nicknames and if our informants have led fairly typical Japanese lives, then Japanese nicknames are relatively non-pejorative and very mild in their implied social criticism. This fits with the general picture we have of Japanese social life, where it seems a strong emphasis is put on public forms of politeness despite the intensively competitive mode of life of most Japanese. We notice that irony is rare in the use of nicknames. We have a report of only one, namely the use of 'Sensei' (teacher) for someone stupid.

The nickname 'Ainoko'
The changing fortunes of this name encapsulate recent Japanese social history. Traditionally it is used for those who look like Westerners, that is have a strong chin, or a white complexion or round eyes, or all three of these 'Western' characteristics. It is, or was, very insulting and was used in teasing to start chases and fights much as names like 'Ice-cream' (European) and 'Chocolate-drop' (West Indian or Pakistani) are used among British children. The pejorative use seems to have arisen after the Second World War as a way of making insulting reference to the illegitimate offspring of unions between American servicemen and Japanese women, who, one of our informants insists, 'were of very low class'.

But in contemporary Japan its use is becoming more complex. Since a 'Western' appearance is now much admired, and sometimes expensively acquired, 'Ainoko' can now be a nickname with a distinctly positive flavour. But a further turn of the spiral has led to 'Ainoko' being used in a new context as an insulting and pejorative way to express the jealousy of those who do not have much chance to become noted for their 'Western' looks for those who do. This has led to a revival of something of the flavour of the immediately post-war use of the nickname 'Ainoko'.

Arabia

Nicknames flourish among Arabic speakers.* We have chosen an informant from what we believe to be a fairly typical Middle Eastern back-

*We are very grateful to 'El Kandelaft', Mr Amin Baidoun, for a very full discussion of village naming practices. The etymology of his own nickname is uncertain but may have reference to turnips.

ground, a man having contacts both in his home village and in the town where he was educated. More or less everyone in the Middle East has a nickname in childhood, usually created at school, and often confined within the school milieu or amongst a circle of friends. In the cities of 'Arabia' nicknaming does not carry on from school, not even in universities where, if there are nicknames in use, they are brought through from school by old schoolmates who have carried on to university with the person concerned. The exceptions are the regular army where nicknames do continue to be created, and prison.

But in villages, nicknames last for the whole of life, though they are usually acquired and fixed in childhood. As we will demonstrate, they are usually pejorative, to say the least, but it seems that continual use deprives them of their semantic connotations, and they have little effect upon either the life or the reputation of their bearer. Again, as with the school names of urban Arabs, these village names do not generally spread beyond the group of people one might call the local villagers. Among the Middle Eastern nations the Egyptians are thought to be an exception to this general system, in that they are believed to make much more use of nicknames among adults, and to spread old ones and invent new ones, on occasion. We have not been able to check this claim by an independent investigation.

Nicknames seem to be used in Arabia in much the same way as they are used in Britain. They are impolite, but in continual use. They seem to serve the promulgation of social norms, and to be used as a kind of reprimand for the violation of those norms. They are also used in teasing, to start chases, and 'fights'. And they can be used for revenge.

There is a harshness about Arab nicknames by comparison even with the British system. This shows up vividly in the way physical disability is made the subject of a nickname. The system can be laid out as follows:

Physical Characteristics

Disabilities
These include 'El A'raj', the lame one; for which 'El Thelath Arjul', the three-legged one, is an appropriate alternative; 'El Awar', the partially blind one, which may also be used metaphorically for someone who doesn't understand something but persists in arguing about it. Then there is 'El Atram', the deaf and dumb one, again sometimes used metaphorically for someone who is stupid. 'El Abufas' and 'El Aburiha' are used for smelly people. Notice how these names highlight and emphasise the disability, rather than conceal it in an embarrased silence.

Appearance
As in the English system, deviations from what would be taken to be

normal for that group of people are marked out, as for example, 'El Ashkar' and 'El A'bad' for those who are lighter skinned or darker skinned than average respectively. Similarly, 'El Iggdag' and 'El Tawa-lan' point to people shorter or taller than normal. Someone with a big mouth who is also talkative becomes 'El Abushhaf' while someone with a shambling walk is 'El Deb'i', the bear. And, of course, he who wears glasses is either 'El Doctor' and even 'Four-Eyes', 'El Arbayun'.

Personal and Social Characteristics

Those indicative of bad character

Animal names are used as a source, in particular, 'El Dab'i' (the hyena) for a sneak or peeping tom; 'El Sulafa' (the tortoise) for someone slow-moving, but more for a smooth, slippery personality. 'El Animar' (the leopard) is used for someone manly, and alert but bad-tempered. 'El Hanzia' (the pig) refers to someone who is not easily fooled but is also dirty and disagreeable. Other names to mark bad characters come from various sources, for example 'El Matin' (the rotting carcase) for some-one mean; 'El Mayeh' (the liquid) for someone effeminate; 'El Ahbal' (the fool) for someone who pretends to be a fool to gain advantage; 'El Dahbar' (the bighead) someone stupid and vain; 'El Bu'leh' (the large stomach) for a greedy person; and, perhaps the worst of all, 'El Abutnain' for someone both dirty, evil-smelling and greedy; while someone who makes claim to omniscience is called 'El Allama', the professorial one.

Good personality characteristics

These are also sometimes picked out, and seem to be devoid of the irony such names would imply among English children. For example, 'El Abushenab' is a name for a virile, tough sort of person, and derives from its literal translation 'the moustached one'. 'El Abuliz' names a generous person and 'El Mawsou'a' (the encyclopedia) someone who really does know what he is talking about.

Miscellaneous

Nobody is spared a name if he is in any way unusual. A twin is called 'El Nus akl', the half-brained one, while a triplet is just 'El Thulathi' —one-third. Recently borrowed into other parts of the Middle East from Egypt is 'El Hashat', the hashish smoker, for someone who is something of a comedian. A version of this name 'El Hashat (eh)' can be used for both men and women to mark a character given to exag-geration and even lying.

These are, of course, all names for males as the article 'El', universally prefixed, would indicate. Our informants, being men, and describing rather traditional Arab life in the villages, were able only to indicate a few female soubriquets. 'Zara', for example, for someone shorter than usual, and 'Deb'ieh' for someone with an ungainly walk, the feminine form of the male 'El Deb'i', the bear.

Spain

Nicknaming is very common in Spain, particularly in rural areas. We collected these nicknames in the Catalan area of northern Spain. The etymology and modes of formation are very similar to those we have already described in use among the children of other cultures. The main categories are as follows:

Names Formed from Physical Appearance

We give just one or two examples in each case, to give the flavour of the system.

A particularly small fourteen-year-old was the possessor of the nickname 'Tapon'. This is the Spanish meaning the sort of cork that you put in the neck of small medicine bottles. Another was called 'Conguito'.

Someone who looked like one of the old Moors was called 'Moreno'.

Names Derived from the Official Name

As in the English case these seemed to be the most numerous of the nicknames.

Contractions
The surname 'Buxareu' is shortened to 'Buxi'; the Christian names 'Javier', 'Joaquin' and 'Ricardo' are shortened to 'Javi', 'Quini' and 'Ricki' respectively.

Phonetic analogy
The surname Damaré becomes associated with the similar sounding word 'Dama' which is used to mean a rich lady.

Sequential transformations
Some of these pieces of word-play, however, are much more complex than their English counterparts. In this area of Spain there are *three* languages spoken: Spanish; Catalan (the 'local' language, which has

been going through a period of intensive revival since Franco's death); and some French, since France is only on the other side of the Pyrenees. The Catalan surname Bellsolell becomes 'Bellosol' *via* the French *'beau soleil'*. The surname (also Catalan) 'Villanova' which can be translated as 'new town' becomes the *Spanish* term for 'old town'. The Catalan 'nova' (Spanish, 'neuva') becomes the Spanish 'vieja' ('old'). Thus, Señor Villanova becomes 'Villavieja'—and changes from Catalan to Spanish in the process. (For a detailed description, see Pitt-Rivers, 1954.)

Eke-names in a Ceylon School During the 1930s

By way of contrast we have the following account:

There was nothing of great significance in the nicknames used in school. They referred mostly to the food generally eaten by an ethnic group or other characteristic factor. Sinhalese boys had to suffer being called 'jak seed fellows' or 'rice gruel fellows'. Ceylon Tamils were appropriately called 'palmyra nut fellows' because the palmyra palm is about the only tree that grows well in Jaffna where most of the Tamils live. Indian Tamils, on the other hand, were called 'dhal fellows' because dhal or lentils were a major item of their diet. Although somewhat derogatory, these nicknames were not considered objectionable. Caste or religious differences were not referred to because they would be taken as personal insults which would call for some form of physical retaliation. In the case of Moslem boys, however, reference was sometimes made to the fact that they were circumcised.*

Strictly speaking, these are not nicknames in our sense, but operative epithets. In this case they seem to have only a mildly derisive function to demarcate clearly racial and religious boundaries. The apparent absence of name-calling for game-starting suggests that perhaps in the racial atmosphere of the Old Raj these boundaries were perhaps too heavily charged to be safely drawn upon at all.

---

*We owe this account to Bill Delay.

11
Name Autobiographies

Our study so far has been concerned with particular social groups and specific naming practices in those groups. We turn now to the most idiographic and intensive phase of all, a series of autobiographies written or reported to us by people who have had to cope with one or more nicknames. We introduce this here to show those who have not experienced the power of names what it feels like to be nicknamed, and deliberately to play with a name with the sense of the name's social power. But since many people did indeed have nicknames, though they prefer now to forget that they ever had them, we offer these tales as reminders.

'Sewage' : The Affectionate Abusive

It is gratifying to know that I was once called 'Sewage'. What a different world it was for me then. How much things have changed!

It was M.B. who used to call me 'Sewage'. There may have been one or two others, but I don't remember them. I used to sit next to him doing first-form French. He used to spend the lessons drilling out the cement between the bricks of the back wall. His game was up one day when that day's implement—a pencil—shot through into the next classroom at the feet of the teacher.

I don't remember why he called me 'Sewage', but it was not used by him as an offensive term. He would smile wryly as though his invention was as apt as could be. Indeed, of course, I was a likeable boy. I was pleased to have a nickname though because it was conferred on me by a boy I liked a lot. He was very funny—the funniest in the class, I think.

He didn't have names for everybody—for one thing he didn't associate with lots of them. The names he coined were like his mind, that is, like a cesspool. In fact the first time I came across that word was through his parodying of Liverpool. I imagine all our minds were breaking out with symptoms of puberty. In that way 'Sewage' wasn't quirky at all.

He was a destructive kind and disobedient of course. Very clever, but not exactly devoted to the school. He left after O-levels. The last I heard of him he was pasting up posters on the London Underground. Into drugs I think. I asked him once what it was like earning a living and he said his 'mind atrophied'. It struck me that not even sixth-formers went in for such accurate diagnoses, and so he belied what he said.

Perhaps there was something about *me* that I was called 'Sewage'. Did I smell? Probably, but then probably not more than others. How come the name stuck for a year or so? Once, I signed a piece of French work 'Fingers Foley'. The teacher was amused when handing the stuff back. But that self-appointed nickname was never taken up. Not that I wanted it to be taken up, but it could have been. I suppose I wasn't regarded as an arch-criminal by the rest of the class.

This reminds me of when I was about fifteen with a friend doing a charity walk around the bridges of London. It was meant to be a charity walk but Pete O'R. and myself saw it as an opportunity to pick up a few girls. For this purpose, to impress the girls, we adopted the names 'Scar' and 'Wolf'. Now we were surprisingly effective in our endeavour. Unfortunately (or fortunately, depending on whether it is her or his point of view) they were from Blackheath way, the other side of London, so it didn't last very long. However, the names only ever had the one outing and died a natural death. I don't really think our effectiveness was attributable to the rather dramatic nicknames—it was difficult to say them because they didn't fit (to be honest).

It was Pete who gave me my next nickname, 'Sunshine'. This obviously derived from my habit of grinning/smiling a lot. Quite a few people would use that, unless they already knew me by another appellation, usually my surname. At primary school I was 'John'. It was a shock the first day of secondary school to be 'Foley'. Even the friends who came with me called me 'Foley' and I called them 'Lee', etc. The thing about 'Sunshine' was, though at school it was more of a strained vocative, at Pete's home the people had actually formed their opinion of me on the basis of my nickname. I think they still call me 'Sunshine'.

My sixth-form career in nominative terms was notable in that I was a person who did not have a nickname that was in some ways familiar, diminutive or ridiculous. For these were the categories when we didn't use surnames. I was called 'Jay Eff'. It was like being respected and liked. If I had merely been respected it would have been 'Foley'. If I had been just liked it would have been 'Eggy' or 'Fitz'. So it was a sort of cross.

Now people call me 'John' again.*

'Lot', 'Batman', etc. The Nominative Career of a Benedictine Monk

I was called 'Fatty', 'Lot' and 'Skinny' whilst I was at school, all because I was fat. I didn't mind 'Fatty'. I was given 'Lot' and 'Skinny' by masters with a turn for irony and I was less happy about them. I particularly resented 'Skinny' as it was so inappropriate.

Before I entered the Order I was a dentist in the Army. I was even more pompous in those days than I am now. I was called 'Fangs' by one young lady, which I resented as an affront to my professional dignity.

On teaching practice the boys called me 'Batman', because of my Benedictine habit. I was really rather pleased.

'Snob' : A Case of Undeserved Scapegoating, at least, according to 'Snob'

I object slightly because, quite honestly, I do not think that it is true, that is, I do not think that I am a snob. But these days I just laugh at it, because I find it just sick. It is no longer a joke. I have taken it for the past two years. I am not called a snob by the people in Wilberforce House (his own house), who generally know me better, and I am only called 'Snob' by those in 4X (his own form), or in the third and fourth forms. No matter what I do, it always sticks, usually because first impressions tend to stick. If I say a word that the others do not understand they tend to mock me, and call me a 'Snob'. Then, the others usually chime in. Otherwise, I am just mocked for the sake of it by people who are insecure or by people who just do not know any better. Generally it just makes me sick, because I do not think that it is justified and I also think that some people mock me when they also do not think that my nickname is justified; therefore they make me sick too, because they really do not know what they are talking about. I would like to go on, but perhaps some other time. . .

But we can throw some further light on this story. One of our informants in the very same form tells us that there are three groups, socially speaking. There are the Intellectuals, the Moderates and 'those who think they are tough', the Toughs. The Toughs hate both

*We are grateful to John Foley for the candour of his autobiography.

the Intellectuals and the Moderates, but they hate the Intellectuals most. 'They hate anyone who's clever, like Y (our informant who is called 'Snob'), and X who is also foreign. And they mock Z because of his physical features. People take out their physical inhibitions on Z.'

'Pog' : The Cradle Name that Stuck, and Became 'Piggy', a Slot

Some tactless idiot of a guest at my christening pronounced how much I resembled 'a little pink pig'. It was from them that I acquired the variations of the theme (name) of pig. In fact 'Sarah', my christened name, was a strange name to me, except in official circumstances. If my mother had not taken it up in later years and used it consistently it would be no more to me than a number assigned for bureaucratic purposes. As it is, it still doesn't feel part of me.

My father's names for me included 'Pog', 'Pumpernickel' and 'Piglet' amongst others, but my brothers never took up the same theme, although they have never (not even yet) managed 'Sarah'.

It therefore caught on at school when one of my friends noticed a letter for me addressed as 'Darling Piglet' and immediately that became 'Piggy'. I probably was fairly messy and indeed, sometimes purposely (almost) provoked it for general laughter. On one occasion I can remember my best friend ruthlessly trying to make me laugh, and succeeding, while I had a mouthful of milk. The hilarity it caused when I sprayed the table now amazes and embarrasses me. However, there was a piggier side than this, I think, which seemed to be discovered as appropriate to my nickname *after* I was nicknamed so. This was my nose problems; sinus, hayfever, continual colds (probably a little to do with the shock of coming to another country as I have been brought up in Africa). If you snuffle loudly at night in a dormitory you're liable to have all sorts of abuse (and objects) hurled at you.

I then went to another school and for the first year people stumbled about with 'D. . . .' (my surname) or Sarah. But after one year my old best friend turned up at the school and set up the 'Piggy' trend at once. With her it was definitely a mark of affection, I don't know about the others, for still now when she's feeling nostalgic and affectionate in that way, she uses it. I can remember being embarrassed that the cat had been let out of the bag, but I probably grew to like it more as I became more accepted with it.

I lived up to it in that I went armed with my blazer absolutely stuffed with rubbishy treasures and therefore received untidiness marks—but this didn't bother me much as I also came top of the form regularly every year. But I'm unlike the Piggy in *Lord of the Flies,* in that I was also very sporty at school.

Even now in the present I have not closed the book on this nickname for my steady boyfriend gradually took over the name 'Pog' from my father and calls me little else (except 'Sarah' in front of strangers) and what's more he resents anybody else (except my family) using it.

Although now I can feel the significances behind being likened to a pig, I think it was mostly over my head in my younger days. It was welcomed as a way of being accepted and even loved (the need is greater in a boarding-school set-up). People are sometimes shocked or horrified when they hear Nigel calling me 'Pog' but I have long ceased to feel embarrassment and am probably even secretly proud of it. After all, it's close to even becoming famous when there are such activities as 'Pog-baiting', objects such as 'Pog-nests' and a potential book 'How to Handle a Pog'.

Finally, however, I must add that I, too, do not and would not like anybody else other than the 'initiated' (the two men in my life, my father and Nigel) to use my present nickname.

'Polly' : Variations on Being the 'Fat Girl'

I was called 'Polly' from birth. It was given to me by the midwife. 'Polly' is a Scottish name for chubby babies. I dislike it, but it isn't stupid.

But later I got other names. From the age of twelve onwards I was called 'Pear' or 'Pear-shaped'. It was started by my brother and came from the shape of my head and chin, with a neck like a stalk. Then I got 'Irene' from about the age of fourteen. It was from 'Pear-shaped' like this: 'Pear-shaped' to 'Persia' to 'Iran' to 'Irene'. Again, one of my brother's inventions. I truly think he's insane!

I got 'Bus' from the age of eighteen. It started as a suffix on 'Irene' to 'Irenebus' and then shortened to 'Bus'.

I think that 'Pear-shaped', 'Irene' and 'Bus' are all stupid, and I ignore them.

'Ginger-nut'

'Christina Jane Bundy'—this was the name given to me by my parents at birth. Now, just twenty-three years later it forms the prototype for a succession of variations—nine in all. This official title itself, though, was special. I knew the origin of two-thirds of it and it always provided me with a 'little story'.

Bundy? Awful isn't it? Still, it has a history. Apparently it's derived from 'Bond-i', an Anglo-Saxon word meaning 'Unfree, bound to the soil'. As we're a Wiltshire family, I can't help thinking we were originally serfs and one brave Bundy ran away for a year and a day.

'And what does that "C" stand for? I thought your name was Jane.'

'Now, that's a legacy from a stubborn Grandpa. I caused problems as soon as I came into the world by being born at Christmas. I had, according to Grandpa, to have a name indicative of the fact. 'Carol', 'Noelle' were all treated with disdain. 'Christine' was deemed just bearable, and quite passable should the final 'e' be changed for an 'a'. Always a very useful 'ice-breaker' at parties. . . .

But Jane wasn't enough for the social jungle of school. From the age of about six to eight the delights of 'Bandy-Bundy', 'Ginger', 'Rusty' and 'Freckles' all came my way. Without exception these were the names of the playground. Shouted at me across the yard they usually formed the prelude to an enjoyable game of 'Chase' and often 'Fighting' for my taunter was invariably male. The names were used as offensive weapons to annoy—and they invariably did. At first my counter-attack was spontaneous—I disliked the names intensely but gradually they became the tacitly accepted ritual before 'Chase', etc. I even earned myself the enviable title 'Best Fighter in the Infants'.

It was in the summer of my ninth birthday that nicknames took on more kindly overtones. I've forgotten his name unfortunately, but it was one of those heart-stopping, breath-taking, whirlwind romances. . . .He stayed in the caravan next door and used to come and ask my Mum, pleadingly: 'Is Ginger-nut coming out to play, please?' I was secretly ever so pleased. As he was the only person to call me this it meant, even then, that we were a special 'twosome'. It seemed, somehow, protective, too.

1963 was a rather traumatic time. We moved house. A new home, new school, a new set of friends. I can remember thinking the least painful way in would be a much more subdued person than I had been; and that I'd like to be 'Copper' in this new set-up. It had nicer, more muted connotations than the slightly abrasive 'Chase'-starters; to be called it would mean I was 'in', but there was more than that. The name conjured up a person—a friendly, quite popular girl, who people respected because of a core of stability underneath. Very well, I have always been a fanciful person. By the way, this plan never succeeded. I was always 'Jane'.

Since then, and only comparatively recently, I have earned myself two more. Both I was quietly pleased with. Not only to me do they smack of a total, social acceptance, they seemed intrinsically comfortable. 'Bundle' came from 'Bundy'—once again a more homely, kindly, variation; while 'Bubbles' derived from a sudden headful of curls. Yet, knowing this, I still took it as a compliment to my sociability and tended to become even 'bubblier' (and more unbearable) in the company of that group.

'U.S. Orgreaves' : An Example of Florid and, Some Would Say, Unnecessary Elaboration

My name is Hargreaves. But I had to appear in the Magistrates Court over the matter of a bald tyre. This seemed far too minor an offence according to my friends, who reckoned 'U.S.I.'—Unlawful Sexual Intercourse—would be that I should really be up for. So I got 'U.S. Orgreaves' as a result.

[We think that this innovation is unlikely to last beyond the Oxford Term in the course of which it was invented.]

Several interesting points emerge from these examples, confirming our objective analyses of the subjective experiences and interpretations of the participants. It is clear:

1   That many people who have nicknames have several transitions from one to another marking a fairly clearly defined social history. Each name marks a specific social relation.

2   There is evidence of a clear understanding of the image-forming and sustaining force of nicknames. Definite personas are seen as sought for and amplifiable through a specific name. Notice the perceived force of 'Scar' and 'Wolf' in the game of picking up girls, and the role of 'Copper' in the plan of the efforts to be put in by a red-headed girl to present herself as a particular kind of person. Notice, too, that self-selected nicknames do not usually stick.

3   Finally, it is clear that slotting is a real social, psychological phenomenon, as we see how 'Piggy' made a necessity of virtue, and took advantage of her nickname to licence her untidiness and other piggish habits. It is also clear that, as she grew up and left these behind, the intimacy that the name implied for her became itself a socially and psychologically sustaining relationship.

12
Miscellaneous Naming Practices

In this chapter we bring together a miscellany of naming practices that seem to us of interest. Each poses a problem that suggests the possibility of further research, if naming as such were the focus of attention.

We print in full a very elaborate scheme for naming friends and acquaintances that exploits both a quite shrewd analysis of character and a joking analogy. It is much the most elaborate personal scheme we have come across, and perhaps enjoyable for its own sake. We think it unlikely that even a tight-knit science sixth-form could sustain such a scheme as a social unit, though we would be interested to know of any cases where something of the sort has worked, even if only for a short time.

The most important distinction is that between boson and fermion. In general, it is a bad thing to be a boson. Since bosons 'prefer' to be in the same quantum state, they are evidently gregarious, not particularly discriminating in their choice of friends, or perhaps discriminating for the wrong reasons. Thus, someone like Mr Weston in *Emma* ('. . . a little less of open-heartedness would have made him a higher character. . .') would be a boson, so would a snob, or a careerist, or possible a Don Juan – though this can also correspond to electrical neutrality. I also use the term to refer to people who I can well do without. This corresponds, rather loosely, to the fact that there are no absolute rules on number conservation for bosons. I often use it this way in speaking of a group of people who all seem more or less alike, and whom I don't know well and don't think I want to: 'Imperial College is full of grotty pions.' Fermions, on the other hand, are exclusive, detached, austere, individualist (not more than one in a given quantum state). They stand out from the crowd. Moreover, all fermions must have a spin of at least $\frac{1}{2}\hbar$. Spin is another important property. When I started to classify people according to spin, it had nothing to do with particle physics, but was in imitation of a peculiarity of G.H. Hardy. According to C.P. Snow, 'Hardy's friends. . .had to pass some of his private tests: they needed to possess a quality which he called "spin" (this is a cricket term, and untranslatable: it implies a certain obliquity or irony of approach). . . .' I agree that the quality is indefinable, though I am not sure that I mean by it exactly the same as Hardy. The best that I can do is to say that it involves intelligence, a certain amount of fastidiousness, a lack (or at least a potential lack) of conventionality, and the ability to be cynical and a little bitchy. Perhaps it can be seen that it is the sort of property one would expect fermions to possess. Bosons must have integral spin, and so, while it is in fact possible for some bosons to have more spin than most fermions (photons and vector mesons have spin $\hbar$ for example), they can also have spin zero, which makes them very boring indeed. To be classified as a pion, kaon, or eta meson (all these are spinless) is therefore rather damning, though the finite spin of vector bosons may go a long way towards their redemption.

Fermions can be further sub-divided into leptons and baryons. These sub-groups are distinguishable in two ways: first, according to the masses of the particles comprising them—there are only four leptons (and four antileptons), all of which have mass less than the proton mass, while baryons have mass greater than or equal to the proton mass—and second, according to the types of inter-actions these particules can undergo:—leptons can only undergo weak or electro-magnetic interactions, while baryons can participate in strong interactions as well. The mass of a particle does not, unfortunately, correspond to anything so objective as the mass of the person in question; few things in this scheme are so straightforward as that. Someone's 'mass' depends on the extent to which he or she makes on me a certain impression of solidity, either physical or intellectual. Someone who seems to have things fairly well sorted out for themselves—whom I might describe as 'serene' and 'wise' if those were words of mine—would be 'massive'. The possible interactions of a particle correspond fairly obviously to the sorts of relationships it forms. It might be thought that in this case leptons would be rather isolated, unable to form close friendships (absence of strong interactions), but to a rather bad approximation, the electromagnetic interaction may be taken as being as strong as the strong interaction, so that it is only neutrinos—uncharged leptons with almost no interaction with matter—which are really to be pitied. I don't think I know any neutrinos; perhaps Bartle- by the Scrivener would be one. Classification according to mass is on the whole the more important in my scheme, since, as I said, the inability to undergo strong interactions need not be very significant.

Bosons are subdivided into photons (of zero mass) and mesons (of finite mass). Photons, which have spin $\hbar$, correspond particularly well, I think, to social climbers and arrivistes, since their speed (that of light) will enable them to go far. Among the various types of meson, classification is primarily according to spin. Vector mesons mostly have greater mass than pseudoscalar (spinless) mesons; this is convenient, since, as indicated, massive particles generally elicit admiration from me (sometimes given grudgingly), and the spin of a vector meson makes it likely that he or she will have some quality —if not precisely wisdom or serenity, then perhaps confidence, or self-possession—which I can admire.

An important type of particle which I have not mentioned yet is the quark. Identifying people with quarks immediately causes problems, since hadrons (baryons and mesons) are believed to be made up of quarks, and it is not possible to incorporate this fact into the scheme. None the less, there are people who simply could not be anything but quarks. Unfortunately, it is difficult to say much more than that. Quarks are fermions, of spin $\frac{1}{2}\hbar$, charged, strongly interacting, and thought to be very massive; they have all the properties that this would imply, but it is hard to pinpoint exactly what it is that their 'quarkness' lies in. A great deal of self-confidence (real or apparent) and pushfulness seems to be a characteristic of quarks— but this could simply be a consequence of their very high mass. Quarks tend to be slightly bewildering people; one is often a little puzzled or over-powered by them, especially on first meeting them, and unsure how to react to them. This, I suppose, reflects the fact that there is still no satisfactory theory of quarks. They may appear eccentric, or, indeed, completely insane—this generally being because they rather like to be thought so, this too is consistent with the fact that quarks have some unusual and as yet unexplained properties.

As well as the strength of the possible interactions a particle can undergo, their range must be taken into account. The electromagnetic interaction is of infinite range, while the strong interaction is of range 10^{-15} m, and the weak interaction is of such short range that it was originally considered to take place at a point. (Actually, the range and 'inherent strength' of the weak interaction are connected, but I ignore this complication.) Thus, the range of a particle's interactions will depend partly on its charge since charged particles can evidently take part in electromagnetic interactions. Charged particles would therefore be likely to form long-lasting friendships—or, at least, to want to do so—while neutral particles, though often charming and agreeable when one is with them, tend to forget one, and to interact instead with whoever happens to be within their range, when one has got away. A certain philanderer of my acquaintance, for example, who undergoes a great many strong interactions at very short range, is thus obviously a neutron. (However, there is still hope that he may interact electromagnetically through his magnetic dipole moment.) It might be thought that the adjustment of positive and negative charge so that people who get on well 'attract' each other would be impossible without inconsistency; but in fact the problem only arises in cases where leptons are involved, since hadrons of the same charge can still interact strongly, and so far there is only one really bad disagreement with observation — the case of a muon and an electron who are the best of friends.

Strangeness does not correspond to eccentricity, though perhaps it ought to, but to homosexuality. I am not sure now that this really deserves a quantum number of its own; but, after all, 'strange' is reminiscent of 'queer'. No distinction is made between negative and positive values of strangeness, but degrees of strangeness can be allowed for; thus omega hypersons have $S = -3$, xis have $S = -2$, and sigmas and lambdas have $S = -1$. Sometimes particles lose their strangeness as they grow up; this, of course, constitutes a weak decay. I know of one, for example, who decayed from a sigma to a proton over a period of a few months. Unfortunately I don't know what would correspond to the phenomenon of 'associated production' (i.e. the creation of strange particles only in pairs, of equal and opposite strangeness) and, though 'strangeness oscillations' are easier to imagine, I've never actually observed any. The increased acceptance of 'strangeness' in recent times, though, surely has its counterpart in the discovery that part of the strong interaction is invariant under rotations SU(3) transformations, or 'Strangeness–independent'.

Charm corresponds simply to charm. However, the particle in question has to be very charming indeed to be thought worthy of being assigned non-zero charm (most fermions, and even some vector bosons, are fairly charming in the usual sense of the word.) From what I have said about massiveness, it will be seen that it is no accident that particles with charm are predicted to be extremely massive. No charmed particles have yet been isolated (in bubble-chamber experiments etc., I mean; I myself have discovered two).

The final distinction that must be made is that between particle and anti-particle. Anti-particles are not simply particles which I am anti — 'some of my best friends are anti-particles' — and in fact they are generally people whom I like, and enjoy the company of, at least for as long as I see them, but whom, for a variety of reasons, I feel hostile towards, or irritated by, when they are absent. This is not as illogical as it sounds, after all, particles do attract their anti-particles in many cases, due to their opposite charge, though since they tend to annihilate each other, the interaction cannot be purely friendly.

There are some quantum numbers which have no place in this scheme at all; isospin, for example, or parity. The lifetimes of particles have also not been considered, though it is interesting that most of my acquaintance do in fact turn out to be protons or electrons, as might be expected on grounds of stability. Apart from the weak decays mentioned above, transformations of one particle into another also have not been incorporated. The difficulties here are obvious; my weakly decaying friend, for example, should have given birth to a pion in the course of her decay. There are a great many other omissions: for example, no account has been taken of the fact that many of the more massive baryons are thought to be simply excited states of lower lying ones, or of the tendency of particles to dissociate into groups of virtual particles. Although I have tried to use the scheme in predictions, its power is really only classificatory; and even then it is something of a private language, as I expect the Reader has gathered only too well.*

Fantasy creations

Lindy

My sister invented Lindy, although at the time (when she was somewhere between the ages of nine and eleven) she would always deny hotly any suggestion that Lindy was in any way less than a 'real person'.

Lindy lived on my grandfather's farm in North Wales—it was almost as if she were one of the children from one of the neighbouring farms, who were themselves creatures of mystery to us people from a less pastoral environment. My sister never mentioned Lindy when we were at home in Cheshire, or with adults, but wherever we walked together about the fields of the farm, my sister was sure to spot Lindy and we would have to go and meet her. I can remember the thing that made me at least half believe in Lindy was the immense amount of detail which my sister managed to put into every supposed description about Lindy. We would be coming to the shadowy corner of some field towards evening, when suddenly my sister might say, 'Look. . .Lindy's been here. . .'

'How do you know?' I would ask.

'You see the way the grass has been bent over here, and look at that scrap of paper there—that's Lindy's all right. . . .'

Suddenly thinking that two could play at this game, I would look around for myself. I can remember on one occasion finding a piece

*This scheme was devised by Caroline Fraser.

of rotting green shoe on the edge of the field and pointing it out to my sister. I said, 'That shoe there – I'm sure it's Lindy's'.

'No, it isn't—Lindy doesn't wear shoes like that—that shoe was left behind by the Gypsies. . .' (The gypsies were also a rather shadowy collection of sinister figures in our childish imaginations.) Whenever I tried to join in the Lindy game I was always told that I was wrong, or that I was 'just trying to make things up'. It was as if Lindy were some sort of spirit creature who needed my sister as a medium to make her presence felt. I just didn't have the gift of being such a medium, so it was never I who saw Lindy for myself. I would always just miss seeing her as she disappeared behind some hazel tree or behind a barn. I never did catch the sound of her voice calling to us, or detect for myself her many and ingenious calling-cards—but my sister did.

Razine, Bambora and Quinar

Between the ages of three and seven Elizabeth Jane had a companion [like 'Lindy'] called 'Hobby'. His name was derived from a highly favoured but ramshackle hobby-horse. But he was clearly not identical to, nor yet wholly different from, the original material embodiment of Hobby in plastic and wood. She invented a biography for him and would open each new chapter with the words 'When Hobby was a little boy. . .'.

'Hobby' and 'Lindy' seem to us very much in the mould of the companions most imaginative children create for themselves. Their names seem to derive from a transfer from a real thing or person to the fantasy creature. But in this case we have an actual invention of novel names for a second kind of fantasy creature, examples of which inhabited different places familiar to the child.

Our informant goes on:

Something called 'Razine' lived in the metal chain connecting the bath plug to its retaining ring, and a creature called 'Bambora' lived under the stairs. These creatures were entirely benevolent. They were of only momentary but repeated interest. They had no biographies and persistent attempts to encourage stories about them comparable to the very elaborated history of 'Hobby' were met with indifference. Finally, there was a creature called 'Quinar'. He had some unspecified connection with the horses who were kept in a neighbouring paddock.

All four creatures dissolved about the same time, when the child was about seven.

We have not been able to establish a plausible etymology for the three supernumerary beings, nor have we come across any parallel cases, which we could study in detail. The odd thing to our ear is how highly differentiated and quite plausible the three names are, and yet they seem to be free inventions. We would be interested in records of any other cases of free creation of names on this scale and with this degree of verisimilitude, from which some clue as to any systematic creative patterns might emerge.

Names for Things

There is a widespread practice among children of naming familiar things with suitable human names. We illustrate this practice with an example. The etymology is by a simple internally motivated formation, the commonest method for finding eke-names. A teacher reports that when a school camp was arranged (which occurred annually), the children used special names for all items of equipment. 'I suspect that the system may have been adult in origin, but it was certainly universally used, and equally certainly children did create names for new things in my hearing.'

The basic rule of the system is that the object is given a christian name whose initial sound is the same as the name of the object (which acts as a sort of surname):

Polly Primus; Priscilla Primus; Penelope Primus, etc. (each primus stove had its own characteristics, although the differences between them were probably undetectable to the uninitiated. All name users, however, were competent at discriminating between them).

Mervyn the Morgue (a sort of huge mallet for knocking marquee pegs in).

Marmaduke Mallet (and a collection of others).

There were two axes—the smaller of the two was called 'Mummy Axe' whilst the larger was called 'Daddy Axe'.

Impropriety in Naming

A student offers us the following anecdote:

I recently went on a computer programming course in Oxford. During the first lecture our attention was drawn to a television screen on which the current state of the computers is displayed. The notice read, 'I am up and running, George.' It seemed reasonable that a computer should be called by a human name. The hardware and software are in some ways analogous to a human body and mind. But then we were told that George (whose name is derived from 'General Organisation of the Environment') is only a programme. The giving of a human name to a series of instructions and pieces of information seemed extremely incongruous and comparable to singling out certain human responses (like saying 'Thank you') and having them rather than the whole person christened.

Appendix 1
The Nicknaming of Teachers

Introduction

Perhaps the use, *sotto voce*, of a naming device normally used for intimacy or to express disapproval and contempt is a way of reducing a powerful person's status to manageable proportions. In this way, in the mind at least, the felt powerlessness of being a pupil is remedied. But whether this is so we are unable to say. We can state with confidence that the nicknaming system in use in a school pretty accurately reflects the social and psychological relations that pupils see as obtaining between themselves and the teaching staff, and represents the reputation in pupil opinion of each teacher. These devices are as widespread in large, diffuse and socially open comprehensives as in tightly knit, closed, private boarding schools.

The System

If nicknames do reflect social norms then one might expect to be able to identify those features of teachers' appearance and behaviour that stand out in the eyes of the pupils. We made detailed comparisons between the systems used in two very different English secondary schools —a coeducational county comprehensive, let us call it 'Wheatfields', and a single-sex urban private school, formerly a famous direct grant high school, let us call it 'Camchester Grammar'. Marked differences did appear in the basis of the nicknaming of teachers.

These figures are obtained (p. 144) from a comparison of the name-categories of teachers who were nicknamed. In Wheatfields every teacher had some form of eke-name, either a nickname proper or some form of contraction or distortion of the given or surname, while in Camchester Grammar 15 per cent of the teaching force were without any pupil-given name at all.

	Wheatfields *per cent*	*Camchester Grammar* *per cent*
Internally motivated names	50	46
Externally motivated names		
(i) physical appearance	22	28
(ii) biographical incident	28	2
(iii) personality	nil	24

The actual system for creating names is pretty much the same as the children use for naming each other. Our data is derived from a wide sample of secondary schools of various kinds in different parts of the country and shows a quite strong uniformity of semantic and etymological trends. The unacceptably different are stigmatised. A man who stinks of stale pipe smoke is 'Pongo' while one with large ears is 'Flapper' and someone very short is 'Titch'. And there are the irresistible opportunities like 'Mr Peppard' to 'Mr Saltard', and 'Miss Wright' to 'Lefty'.

We have already mentioned the inheritance of nicknames by successive members of a family. The same occurs with teachers' nicknames. We have a record of a Mr W., the third generation of his family to teach in a particular county school, each of which was called 'Daggle'. Office can also serve as the basis for transmission. We have the following account illustrating this:

I spent some time teaching 'Divinity' in an independent boarding school. As the school was not large, this meant that not only did the School Chaplain and myself have a monopoly on Religious Education between us, but also, being a boarding school, I became a sort of honorary assistant Chaplain. At first I was puzzled by the name 'Puppy' which I received, especially so when it became apparent that my predecessor in this role had been given the same name. After some digging around, I managed to unearth the etymology of the name, which goes something like this:

Anglican clergymen wear the traditional clerical collar, which itself has acquired the nickname of 'dog-collar'. The school Chaplain wore a dog-collar and was sometimes referred to amongst the pupils as 'The Dog'. It is then but a short step to say that the assistant Chaplain (a lesser creature than the Chaplain) should be given a diminutive form of the word 'Dog'—and so I was christened 'Puppy'.

An important category of names having no analogue in the children's autonomous worlds are informal titles. The headmaster is often called 'the old man', or 'the boss', though rather surprisingly we have no records of any called 'the gaffer'. Headmistresses, so far as we have knowledge of the matter, either have a traditional nickname or none at all. We owe to Jonathan Bye the report of a person who was known in his school-teaching days as 'the sir', though other teachers in that school had ordinary kinds of nicknames and other appellations.

Much the same system operates on the Continent. We illustrate with two examples from Belgium. The successor of a long-reigning head-master called *Clou* was always known as *Chasse Clou*. A rich example of biographical incident and personality making is reported from Antwerp where a teacher well known for his admiration for a textbook by *Chlovsky* became known as 'Slovski', from the Flemish word *slof*, meaning 'slippers', a tribute to his rather gliding walk and his gentle, ingratiating personality.

Speculative Commentary

It is clear that the comfortable adage repeated by many an unpopular teacher that nicknames reveal affection, is not true. More apposite is the principle of exorcists that it is easier to cast out a devil whose name you know than one who is anonymous. Most nicknames for teachers are rather nasty. We instance 'Bare bum', 'Cow pat', 'Feeble' and 'Lemonlegs' from among hundreds, all internally motivated but developed in a derogatory and hostile direction. There are some principles at work with considerable social loading.

Type-casting

While the names by which children label their teachers are again reflective of the child's interaction with his social environment, the 'flat character' implied in the nickname may well approach the reality of the teacher in the classroom. For one of the major reasons why teachers are such a ready butt for nicknaming is that they often find it expedient to project a stereotyped image of themselves within the classroom. This may be as a protective measure, a defence against the children, or it may be because the expectations of the school, parents and even the children, force the teacher into presenting himself in a particular role. Whatever the factors involved, a teacher's behaviour within the school often facilitates a stereotyping nickname.

Teacher's Awareness and Use of His or Her Own Nickname

Since the nicknames which children use for teachers often virtually define the 'us and them' nature of schools, teachers are rarely called by their nickname to their faces and similarly children often strongly resent a teacher using a child's nickname. Occasionally, however, a teacher will encourage the use of a nickname applied to himself, particularly, of course, if it furthers the image which he wishes to project. ('I remember being taught by a P.E. teacher, a cruel and sometimes vicious man, who revelled in his nickname "Thuggy" and openly encouraged its use'.) Nevertheless, the earlier remarks concerning the self-fulfilling prophecy of nicknames among children may also be applied to teachers and their nicknames. Usually the first realisation by a child or class, that a teacher is aware of his nickname, and those of his colleagues, comes as something of a revelation and may well constitute an important step in the child's conceptualisation of the teacher as an individual.

Transformation with Intimacy

There is a common tendency among schoolchildren to nickname the most popular teachers simply by their christian names, or an affection-ate form of their surname, such as 'Old Smithy'. This practice generally tends to become more marked the higher one goes up the school, which, it can be assumed, is the result of the child's more varied ex-perience of the teacher forcing him to recognise a complex reality be-hind the simplifying nickname. One of our informants, a sixth-former, pointed out that while these names were used by the younger children, sixth-formers tend to address the teachers by their christian name or (less often) by surname, occasionally to the teacher's face. How much of this change of perspective is due to the development of the child, however, and how much to the change from formal classroom teaching in favour of a more personal approach in the sixth form, is open to speculation.

In a parallel and very detailed study of the nicknames in use in a large comprehensive school in a different part of the country from the two schools we used for the basic comparisons above, we looked for a cross-check on the methods by which respect was ritually marked in naming. We were able to show very clearly that respect and affection for the established teacher is marked by the use of the teacher's given name as the regular means of referring to him behind his back and *sotto voce*, no matter how tempting the surname or weird and eccentric the personality or bizarre the personal appearance.

However, some teachers who are particularly liked or respected pass through that stage to what one might call a kind of nominative apo-theosis with such nicknames as 'Mighty Midget' for a short, energetic and highly admired deputy headmaster, and 'Granny' for a stern but much respected remedial teacher.

Non-persons

There are, of course, the teachers who appear to the children shadowy and uninteresting and consequently do not receive a nickname. For although these nicknames are not dependent upon the affection generated by a teacher, they may well be a measure of his personality. Such unnamed figures are instead often referred to rather contemptuously by their surname. It seems reasonable to suggest that these teachers have failed to become fully digested into the social life of the school.

Finally, to revive the flavour of it all for those of our readers who have forgotten their school days, we append two lists from two more, but again very different schools.

(a) From a rural comprehensive: here are the teachers fortunate enough to be educating the fourth form:

'Monty', 'Funky', 'Twich', 'Mildew', 'Fluster', 'Scotch Krotch', 'Peri-cycle', 'Maud', 'Baby-face', 'Earthworm', 'Sexy', 'Rubberchops', 'Frost arse', 'Fruity', and 'Frustrated Parrot'.

(b) From a traditional 'public-school: six well-known masters go under the following:

'Boggo': this name was given to a master with wiry hair and who smoked continuously. He presented, in his own person, two of the salient features marked by the use of that name among the boys themselves. (Cf. Ch. 6).

'Bunji': the interesting thing about this name was that there was a 'folk' explanation which was both widely held and totally erroneous. The common belief was that most people who used the name thought that it was a sort of onomatopeoic word derived from the sound the master's soft-soled shoes made whilst he walked about the corridors. The real explanation, given to us by a boy fairly high in the school's hierarchy, was that it formed quite simply from the little-known middle name of the master – Benjamin.

'Bush': A master with an unusually fine set of eyebrows.

'Garibaldi': A master who was beginning to lose his hair. Also abbreviated to 'Gary'.

'Doc. Choc.': One of the teaching staff, armed with his doctorate, spent some time in Africa, from whence he acquired a prominent sun-tan.

'Rabbit': The usual prominent front teeth. No originality here.

Appendix 2
Adult Nicknames

The following is a sample of the nicknames used by adults in a large ship-building yard:

'Sheriff': Name given to a foreman whose catch-phrase on finding idling men was 'What's the hold-up?'

'Haversack': Name given to another foreman—'. . .because he's always on my back.'

'Bungalow': Name given to a man because popular opinion had it that there was 'nothing upstairs'.

'Balloon': Given to one who was reputed to be fond of the phrase, 'Don't let me down'.

'Pawnbroker': 'Leave it to me lads.'

'The Parson': only works on Sundays, when he can get double time.

This list gives us a brief glimpse of character appraisal among adults. We include it here in the hope that someone may be encouraged to use nickname analysis to explore the norms of appearance and behaviour operative in those places in the adult world that are sufficiently socially closed to have developed their own moral systems.

Bibliography

Argyle, M. (1976), 'Personality and social behaviour', in R. Harré (ed.), *Personality* (Oxford, Blackwell), Ch. 6.

Barley, N.F. (1974), 'Perspectives on Anglo-Saxon names', *Semiotica*, vol. II, pp. 1–31.

Barstow, S. (1973), *Joby*, (London, Corgi).

Bowlby, J. (1971), *Attachment and Loss*, vol. I, (Harmondsworth, Penguin).

Brittan, A. (1973), *Meaning and Situations* (London, Routledge & Kegan Paul).

Bruner, J. (1977), Address to Social Psychology Workshop, Oxford University, Nov. 1977.

Busse, T.V. and Helfrich, J. (1975), *J.Psych*, vol. 89, pp. 281–3.

Cumming, E. (1967), 'The name is the message', *Trans-Action*, vol. 4, pp. 50–2.

Ellis, A. and Beechley, M. (1954), 'Emotional disturbance in children with peculiar given names', *J.Genet.Psych*, vol. 85, pp. 337–9.

Fagelson, O.W. (1946), 'Students' reactions to given names', *J.Soc. Psych*, vol. 23, pp. 187–95.

Finch, M., Kilgren, H. and Pratt, K.C. (1944), 'The relation of first name preferences etc.', *J.Soc.Psych*, vol. 20, pp. 249–64.

Fraser, R. (1973), *The Pueblo* (London, Allen Lane), p. 134.

Goffman, E. (1961), *Asylums* (New York, Doubleday and Co.; Harmondsworth, Penguin, 1968).

Goffman, E. (1963), *Stigma* (Harmondsworth, Penguin).

Golding, W. (1972), *Pincher Martin*, (London, Faber).

Hargreaves, D.H. (1967), *Social Relations in Secondary Schools* (London, Routledge & Kegan Paul).

Harré, R. (1976), 'Living up to a name' in R. Harré, (ed.), *Personality* (Oxford, Blackwell), ch. 3.

Harré, R. (1977), 'Friendship as an accomplishment', in S. Duck, (ed.),

Theory and Practice in Inter-Personal Attraction (London and New York, Academic Press), ch. 17.

Hartmann, A. A., Nicoley, R. C. and Hurley, J. (1968), 'Unique personal names as a social adjustment factor', *J.Soc.Psych,* vol. 75, pp. 107-10.

Hollander, E. P. and Hunt, R.G. (1972), *Current Perspectives in Social Psychology,* (New York, Oxford University Press).

Jahoda, G. (1954), 'A note on Ashanti names and their relation to personality', *Brit.J. of Psych,* vol. 45, pp. 192-5.

Lambert, R. (1968), *The Hothouse Society* (London, Weidenfeld & Nicolson).

Le Carré, J. (1976), *Tinker, Tailor, Soldier, Spy,* (London, Pan), pp. 16-17.

Levy-Bruhl, L. (1976), *Notebooks on Primitive Mentality* (Oxford, Blackwell).

Lewis, M. M. (1969), *Language and The Child* (Windsor, NFER).

McDavid, J.W. and Harrari, H. 'Social desirability of names', unpublished paper.

Mortimer, J. (1973), 'David and Broccoli', in *Conflicting Generations* (London, Longmans).

Opie, I. and Opie, P. (1959), *The Lore and Language of Schoolchildren* (London, Oxford University Press).

Partridge, E. (1959), *Name this Child* (London, Hamish Hamilton), (6th reprint, 1974).

Peevers, B. H. and Secord, P. F. (1974), 'The development and attribution of person concepts', in *Understanding Other Persons,* Mischel, T. (ed.), (Oxford, Blackwell), pp. 117-42.

Pitt-Rivers, J.A. (1954), *The People of the Sierra* (London, Weidenfeld & Nicholson), pp. 160-9.

Richards, M.P.M. (1974), *The Integration of a Child into a Social World* (Cambridge University Press), Ch. 5.

Rossi, A.S. (1965), 'Naming children in middle class families', *Am.Soc. Rev,* vol. 30, pp. 499-513.

Savage, B.M. and Wells, F. L. (1948), 'A note on singularity in given names', *J.Soc.Psych,* vol. 127, pp. 271-2.

Secord, P. F. and Backman, C. (1972), *Social Psychology* (New York, McGraw-Hill), (revised edition).

Shotter, J. (1979), *The Making of a Person* (London, Routledge & Kegan Paul).

Sluckin, A. (1978), *Life in the Playground* (doctoral dissertation: Oxford University).

Strauss, A. (1972), *Language in Education* (Open University Publications).

Vygotsky, L. (1962), *Thought and Language* (Cambridge Mass. MIT Press).

von Hagen, V.W. (1973), *The Ancient Sun Kingdoms of the Americas* (London, Paladin), p. 41.

Waterhouse, K. (1968), *There is a Happy Land* (London, Longmans).

Whorf, B.L. (1956), *Language, Thought and Reality* (Cambridge, Mass., MIT).

Woulfe, P. (1923), *Irish Names for Children* (London, Gill and Macmillan) (revised edition, 1974).

The following works contain no mention of names or nicknames.

Giglioli, P.P. (1972), *Language and Social Context* (Harmondsworth, Penguin Books).

Giles, H., and Powesland, P.F. (1975), *Speech Style and Social Evaluation* (London, Academic Press).

Pride, J.B. and Holmes, J. (1972), *Sociolinguistics* (Harmondsworth, Penguin Books).

Robinson, W.V. (1972), *Language and Social Behaviour* (Harmondsworth, Penguin Books).

Sandell, R. (1977), *Linguistic Style and Persuasion* (London, Academic Press).

Index